The Heart of the Matter²

A second helping of letters to my children

Ex Libris
Cole Walker
and his friends

52 devotionals for families on the issues of today

Brad Harrub Ph.D.

The Heart of the Matter 2

THE HEART OF THE MATTER 2

Published by Focus Press, Inc.

© Copyright 2019 Focus Press, Inc.
International Standard Book Number

Interior and cover design by: Stephanie Caldwell
Cover image by: Getty Images
Interior images by: Getty Images and Brad and Melinda Harrub

All Scripture quotations are from the New King James Version,
copyright 1979, 1980, 1982,
Thomas Nelson, Inc., Publishers, unless otherwise noted.

Printed in the United States of America

For information or to order copies of
Heart of the Matter 2,
contact the publisher:

FOCUS PRESS, INC.
625 Bakers Bridge Ave, Suite 105
Franklin, TN 37067

Library of Congress cataloging-in-publication
Brad Harrub (1970 -)
Heart of the Matter 2
Includes Biblical references
ISBN: 978-099925576-6
1. Religion. 2. Christian Family. 3. Parenting.
I. Title

Dedication

To Brian and DeAnn

Thank you for sharing your wisdom, sharing your family, and sharing your love. We can never begin to repay you for the blessing you have been to our family.

I look forward to many more island adventures and New Year's in FL.!

Acknowledgements

A book has the author's name on the front, but I learned more than a decade ago that putting a book together requires a host of people. Undoubtedly, as I try to recall all those people I will leave some out, so please forgive me!

Thank you to Tonja and Melinda for proofing the original "Heart of the Matter" articles. While I detest your red pen, I appreciate more than you know your eagle eyes.

Thank you to Stephanie Caldwell for the hours you poured into laying this out and designing the cover. Also, thank you for working with me through my insane travel schedule.

Thank you to our friends at Southern Hills for informal Bible discussions, late night card games, and thousands of texts that helped inspire some of these topics.

Thank you to the readers who encouraged me to keep this series going. You are the reason this book exists.

Thank you to all of my supporters and to those who support Focus Press. Without you I literally could not do what I do.

Thank you to our printer who also puts up with my crazy travel schedule and works with us to provide you with a great finished product!

Thank you to my wife, who puts into practice the words of this book everyday. Thank you for demonstrating through your life what it really means to live a Christian life. I thank God for your passion to get our children to heaven! I love this amazing journey we are on together. Thanks for saying "Yes."

Also, to my four children. When I first started writing these "letters" at least one of you were still in diapers. I am astonished at how quickly time has flown by. I was never sure how long God would keep me on this earth, so I started these letters as a way of preserving my teaching for you. It is my prayer that these letters will be replayed in your heart and maybe passed on to your children one day. Thank you for loving me, even when I mess up. And thank you for honoring me with the title of

"Dad." Never forget your #1 and # 2 goals in life!

Lastly, thank you to our amazing God. You have blessed me far more than I ever deserved. May you receive all the glory and praise!

Brad Harrub

HOW TO USE THIS BOOK

This book was designed so you can use it for weekly studies with your family, friends, or small groups. We purposefully included 52 different topics so that you could schedule one per week. We encourage you to spend 15-30 minutes per week studying not only each topic, but also other related Scriptures. It will be important to identify a specific time (morning or evening) that you can gather and study—and not allow the world to interfere with this time.

We also encourage you to keep a journal and Bible close at hand. As questions come up, write them down in your journal to research or study more in depth at a later period. Spend time looking at additional passages of Scripture and consider how these passages apply to you today. Spend time each week discussing questions and in prayer over each topic presented.

Table of Contents

Personal Life

Cursing — 10
Peer Pressure — 13
Media — 16
Courtesy/Civility — 19
Internet Pornography — 22
Prioritizing your Time — 25
Shacking Up — 28
Relationships — 30
Verbal Abuse — 33
Getting Your Feelings Hurt — 36

Christian Character

Chivalry — 38
Vanity — 41
Longsuffering — 43
Lust — 45
Boldness — 47
Obedience — 49
Finishing the Course — 52
Holiness — 54
Gentleness — 57
Generosity — 59
Self-Control — 61

Church Life

Singing — 64
The 10 Commandments — 66
Angels — 68
Angels Part 2 — 71
The Scariest Verse in the Bible — 74
Works of Righteousness — 77
Being United in Christ — 79
How We Got the Bible — 82
Fasting — 85

Serve Him: Now! 88
Persecution 90

Parenting

This Hurts Me More Than It Hurts You 92
Discipline 95
Adoption 98
Sexual Abuse/Sexual Predators 101
Legacy 103
Socialization 106
Bullying 109
Grandparents 112
In-Laws 114
The Dinner Table 117

Christian Family Life

Evolution 119
Retirement 122
Mission Minded 124
The Fear of the Lord 127
Leaving the Church 130
Identifying the Enemy 133
A Biblical Worldview 136
Feeding Your Soul 139
Absolute Truth 141
Talking About Jesus 143

Cursing

It is getting harder and harder to avoid them — cuss words. We hear them at ball games, we read them in novels, we listen to them on television (even commercials now!), and we see "friends" use them on Facebook. As our society continues to lose its moral footing, our language falls deeper and deeper into the gutter.

Long gone are the days when a single word—as was uttered in *"Gone with the Wind"* — will cause the nation to pause and consider what is moral and right. Instead, we have song lyrics today that would cause many sailors to blush.

So where is the church in all of this profanity? Have we allowed our voices to be heard, or do we just turn a deaf ear? How many times have we heard that the latest blockbuster movie was "really good, except I think it had a few bad words in it."?

The truth reveals many Christians have become desensitized to cursing. The contagion of "potty mouth" has influenced and infected far too many Christian homes today. Add to this that many congregations continue to put on blinders as their young people type obscenities and euphemisms in the public domain of Facebook.

Here's what I intend to teach my children about cursing.

So, it's confession time. There was a time when your dad did not use wisdom in choosing his words. In fact, there was a time that I possessed a potty mouth. It bothers me to say that, but I want you to know the truth and the struggles that I endured with it. I am not proud of it and I am thankful that the blood of Christ is able to forgive the sins of my past! Never forget that once you make the poor choice of incorporating profanity into your vocabulary, it is extremely hard to weed it out. It is better to never start than to have to consciously remind yourself that Christians do not use that language. (This is why we try very hard to filter what is coming into our house!)

There are three categories of cursing/cussing

The first involves cursing God. When the Ten Commandments were handed down to the Israelites, God made sure they understood He would not stand for this. "You shall not take the name of the Lord your God in vain, for the LORD will not hold him guiltless who takes His name in vain." (Exodus 20:7; see also Deuteronomy 5:11). Make no mistake about it—you are not to ever curse God or use His name in a derogatory fashion!

The second category is cursing someone or something. Again, the Bible is very clear that cursing is not something Christians should be doing. There is often a very negative connotation associated with individuals who curse.

Consider passages like Psalms 10:7, "His mouth is full of cursing and deceit and oppression; under his tongue is trouble and iniquity." (See also Psalms 59:12; 109:17; Romans 3:13-18; James 5:12; and Leviticus 19:12). Decisions about eternity belong to God, not us. Use your words very carefully and do not get into the habit of cursing someone or something.

The third category is what we might commonly refer to as cussing or profanity. This one is a little more tricky — kind of like nailing Jell-O to a tree. There is not a specific list of words in the Bible that I can point you to and say, "Do not say those." Our language changes — as does the meaning for some words. What might have been considered profane fifty years ago, may no longer be a word that is used, or it may mean something different. As such, my words to you in this category are to use wisdom and consider your influence.

---

euphemism • noun
eu·phe·mism | \ yü-fə-mi-zəm
: the substitution of an agreeable or inoffensive expression for one that may offend or suggest something unpleasant.

Christians should be conscious of their speech and use it for good. Paul admonished, "Let no corrupt word proceed out of your mouth, but what is good for necessary edification, that it may impart grace to the hearers" (Ephesians 4:29; see also Proverbs 25:11). You will know what words are considered "bad words" and which are not. As Paul urged the church at Colossae, "Let your speech always be with grace, seasoned with salt, that you may know how you ought to answer each one" (Colossians 4:6).

Cursing • Personal Life

11

Ask yourself. Would you use a euphemism in prayer? Why/Why not?

Again, in Paul's letter to the church at Colossae, he reminded the Christians to put off all of these: "anger, wrath, malice, blasphemy, filthy communications out of your mouth." I pray that as you grow and mature you will use your mouth to build up and encourage. Nowadays, when I hear people curse, I often wonder if they choose those words because they have such a poor vocabulary. As the writer of Proverbs said, "The heart of the wise teaches his mouth, and adds learning to his lips" (Proverbs 16:23).

Verses for Further Study

Exodus 20:7	Psalms 109:17	Ephesians 4:29
Deuteronomy 5:11	Romans 3:13-18	Proverbs 25:11
Psalm 10:7	James 5:12	Colossians 4:6
Psalms 59:12	Leviticus 19:12	Proverbs 16:23

Cursing • Personal Life

Peer Pressure

Actions are often the result of influence. We may be influenced by our parents not to pass notes during worship. Or, we may be influenced by our friends to wear particular clothing brands or styles. Likewise, we may be influenced by God — and our promise to be faithful to Him — to do certain things. But, the bottom line is still the same: actions are often a result of influence.

Many individuals call this "peer pressure," a phrase that I've never fully understood because we can certainly be influenced by individuals not in our "peer" group. While it may not be technically correct, the concept is still a good one. When we hear the words 'peer pressure', we almost automatically think of teenagers. In fact, teens hear the phrase and often cringe, rolling their eyes at the very sound of it, thinking: "Not another lesson on drugs or sex." Most do not realize that peer pressure can be a good thing or a bad thing.

Without a doubt, peer pressure has found its way into the church. It often dictates fashion, songs, worship traditions, church programs, and even Bible class material. Sometimes this can result in good things — like spiritual or numerical growth. Other times, it can drive congregations away from their focus on God and spiritual matters.

Here is what I intend to teach my children about peer pressure.

Consider the following scenario: A solid Christian young person is asked to leave a gymnasium filled with his classmates. While he is out in the hallway a teacher instructs the rest of the students to answer a question incorrectly — on purpose — by standing up. The young man is invited back into the gym and the teacher begins teaching. Several minutes later she asks the class a question — to which the young man obviously knows the correct answer. But, he watches as the entire room stands up, supporting the wrong answer. After a few milliseconds of his mind wrestling with himself, and realizing that everyone else is standing, his muscles finally win over and the young man stands up.

He does this even though he knows it is the incorrect answer! This, my children, is peer pressure. Scientifically speaking, it is very real and you will be wrestling with it much of your life.

It takes a strong individual to always stand up for what is right. There will be times in the future that you are negatively "pressured" to drink alcohol, participate in sexual activity, or watch immoral movies. I encourage you to decide right now exactly what you deem right in the sight of God, and determine how you will respond.

As Paul is encouraging the Christians in Ephesus, he urges them, "Put on the whole armor of God, that you may be able to stand against the wiles of the devil." (Ephesians 6:11). He then continues, "Therefore take up the whole armor of God, that you may be able to withstand in the evil day, and having done all, to **stand. Stand** therefore..." (vs. 13ff). Do you notice how often he says "stand"? Does this sound like someone who would give in to negative peer pressure? Standing up for right is an important aspect of our Christian lives.

Think back to some of the Bible accounts we have studied. How often did we read about strong men and women who were willing to stand for that in which they believed? For instance, David could have given into peer pressure on the battlefield against Goliath (1 Samuel 17). Queen Esther went before the King on behalf of the Jews knowing that she could lose her life (Esther 4-5). Or how about Moses, who "refused to be called the son of Pharaoh's daughter, choosing rather to suffer affliction with the people of God than to enjoy the passing pleasures of sin" (Hebrews 11:24-25)? Likewise, we have strong pictures in the Bible of individuals who allowed peer pressure to lead them down the wrong path. Aaron was pressured into making a golden calf by the Israelites who had become impatient waiting for Moses (Exodus 32). Remember, peer pressure is real. Decide now how you will react.

I pray that you learn to stand. Your mom and I are doing our best to help you grow in wisdom and helping you learn how to discern good from bad. But ultimately, the choice will fall to you. Consider what happened when God rehearsed the sins of Jerusalem in Ezekiel 22. After recounting all of the evil that was transpiring, He said, "So I sought for a man among them who would make a wall, and stand in the gap before Me on behalf of the land that I should not destroy it; but I found no one" (Ezekiel 22:30). My prayer is that you will always be ready and willing to stand in the gap!

WITH YOUR FAMILY THINK OF WAYS TO OVERCOME THE INFLUANCE OF THOSE IN YOUR FRIEND GROUP WHO ASK YOU DO TO OR PARTICIPATE IN THAT GO AGAINST YOUR MORALS.

Verses for Further Study

Ephesians 6:11	Hebrews 11:24-25
Ephesians 6:13	Exodus 32
1 Samuel 17	Ezekiel 22
Esther 4-5	

Peer Pressure • Personal Life

Media

Media • Personal Life

Having looked into the tearful eyes of parents whose children have abandoned the Faith, I have learned there are a million miles between our children "going through the motions" in reference to their spiritual lives versus our children possessing hearts that dictate their actions. I plan to share with you what I hope to instill in the hearts of my own children and those whom I love.

Stop for a moment and consider how much media you have ingested in the last week. This diet would include—but is not limited to—television, movies, video games, Internet, advertising, radio, smartphones, etc. Now, consider two things: (1) how has that media influenced you; and (2) was that media glorifying to God? This constant deluge of media in our lives has altered the attention spans of many. We have become a "sound-bite" nation, as media consumers surf from site to site, and movie scenes change quickly to hold the attention of young viewers. Simply put, media has become a dominating force in the lives of most.

Media, in and of itself, can either be good or bad. Many people rely on computers for news on a daily basis.Many young people have become proficient at making homemade videos to share with their friends. But for many, media has become an addiction. Their lives literally revolve around checking emails, texting, playing video games, or watching television.

This constant desire for media has infiltrated its way into the church. Many Bible classes are looking for ways to incorporate more media into the classroom. Numerous faithful Christians have exchanged time that used to be spent in theWord for media time. Few can say that media is not having an impact on the church or the Christian family. In many cases, the increase in media devices has outpaced parents' consideration or rules for their children.

Here is what I intend to teach my children about media.

I truly enjoy listening to older generations share what they did when they were children—back before computers were around. They speak of a time when life seemed to travel at a much slower pace and times were more innocent. For instance, your grandmother has shared with you that she would spend literally hours playing with homemade paper dolls when she was a little girl. Believe it or not, even your dad grew up in an age where we spent much of our time playing outside and computers were relatively absent (okay, so I do remember getting a Commodore 64 and our family eventually got an Atari hooked up to our "one" television).

Times have changed.

New toys and electronics have ushered in many changes—and have sped up the pace of life into a frantic high-speed pursuit of pleasure. In Charles Dickens' book A Tale of Two Cities, he proclaimed, "It was the best of times, it was the worst of times."While that may not seem possible, it accurately describes the position you are in when it comes to media. Right now at your fingertips you have access to more information than any previous generation has ever possessed. You can learn about foreign countries, foreign languages, or research bugs all without ever leaving the living room.

Name some ways you can glorify God with the use of media.

In many ways, it is the "best of times" when it comes to what media offers. However, many of your friends have become dependent on media—so much so that they are unable to carry on a healthy conversation with adults. Young people text rather than talk. Others find more comfort in "virtual" worlds rather than in the lives they are actually living. In addition, while you can learn about all kinds of good things from media, it also acts as a portal for immoral material as well. [Remember the psalmist declared, "I will set nothing wicked before my eyes; I hate the work of those who fall away; It shall not cling to me" (Psalm 101:3).] Indeed, it appears that it is also "the worst of times."

From a fairly young age your mom and I made the conscious decision to limit your intake of media.We did this for multiple reasons, but one was that we wanted to make sure that media did not become an addiction— that instead you spent time outside enjoying God's

Media • Personal Life

17

creation. We wanted to make sure you worship the Creator and not the creation (Romans 1:25). You will find such peace and healing by occasionally "going off the grid." Unfortunately, many people no longer truly meditate on Him and His Word. That meditation must take place in a media-free environment. I believe parents should be teaching moderation when it comes to media.

I pray that as you mature you will limit yourself and will recognize the value of face-to-face relationships. I want you to not only be able to carry on conversations with adults, but to be able to communicate affectively to others about the good news of Jesus Christ.

While the Bible does not have specific "media guidelines," it does have eternal truths about meditating on good things (Philippians 4:8). My goal as your dad is to make sure you learn how to handle media rather than allowing it to handle you—and to demonstrate how to use it for your good. So when I ask you to "turn it off," understand that part of what I'm saying is "turn Him on.

Family Challange

CHALLENGE EACH FAMILY MEMBER TO LIMIT **ALL** MEDIA TO 15 MINUTES PER DAY. CAN YOU DO IT?

Verses for Further Study

| Psalm 101:3 | Romans 1:25 | Philippians 4:8 |

Courtesy/Civility

There was not a precise date that it occurred, like 9/11, but we have all watched it happen gradually through the years. It wasn't something that we could immediately place our finger on and take corrective action, but rather it slowly leached out of society — the lack of common courtesy and civility.

Gone are the days when people would stop to speak to one another on the street or hold doors for strangers. In fact, gone are the days when you can count on getting good service at restaurants or places of business. These have been replaced by individuals who are bustling about and are only considerate of themselves. Words like "thank you" and "please" have been heaped onto the relic pile of history.

While courtesy and civility can still be found within a church family, the fact remains that both are leaching out in the church as well. ("As the home goes, so goes the church.") We hurriedly walk past one another, sometimes without ever saying hello.

In some ways we have sterilized and mechanized our courtesy. Things that individuals used to do out of the kindness of their hearts are now "expected," as we set up committees and groups to handle various acts of kindness. Christians rarely take the time to weep and rejoice with one another as Paul admonished (Romans 12:15). Often our patience and tempers are shorter whereas our excuses to fellowship and care for one another are longer.

Here's what I intend on teaching my children about courtesy and civility.

I'm not sure how your feet can get so dirty! There have been several occasions in which your feet are literally brown from dirt. Now consider for a moment how it felt when Mom would take you (carry you) upstairs and wash those dirty feet in the bathtub. While you probably never considered it, your mother was mimicking the Master

Courtesy/Civility • Personal Life

19

Teacher. Never forget the example Jesus gave His disciples by washing their feet (John 13:1-17). Picture the Son of God reaching into a basin and washing all of the grime off of their feet. Jesus was demonstrating, through His actions, how we should treat one another. Jesus said, "If I then, your Lord and Teacher, have washed your feet, you also ought to wash one another's feet. For I have given you an example, that you should do as I have done to you" (John 13:14- 15). I hope that you never reach the point in your life that you believe others should serve you. While this may be commonplace in society, it is not commonplace in Christian homes.

A society in which people don't look out for one another is not a fun place to live. And yet sadly, I'm afraid this is the society in which you are growing up.

> *And as you would that men should do to you, do you also to them likewise.*
> *~ Luke 6:31*

The Golden Rule (Luke 6:31) has been forgotten as many people seek to serve themselves. Carefully consider these words: "Do unto others as you would have them do unto you." Much of what we observe in people today is from a selfish "I-Me" attitude. I pray that your heart will be pricked any time you exhibit such an attitude.

Your mom and I have tried very hard to mold you in areas such as politeness, respect, and graciousness. I recognize that there will be times you forget or times in which courtesy slips your mind. But let me encourage you to make courtesy a life-long habit. Your efforts will not go unnoticed. Just like your mom and I frequent specific restaurants because of their good service, likewise people will want to be around you if you take the time to show them they are important.

And they are. Never forget that each person you come into contact with has a soul that will one day spend eternity somewhere. Never forget that everyone you meet was made in the image and likeness of God (Genesis 1:26-27)!

A servant attitude will look for ways to be courteous. Reach out and open the door. Help someone pick up things they dropped. Help someone carry groceries to the car. Help your neighbor with a backyard project. Live your life in such a way that people witness the Golden Rule in action.

Courtesy/Civility • Personal Life

Family Discussion

IN WHAT WAY CAN YOU BECOME MORE
CURTIOUS TO FAMILY MEMBERS?
TO CHURCH MEMBERS?
TO COMMUNITY MEMBERS?

Verses for Further Study

Romans 12:15	Luke 6:31
John 13:1-17	Genesis 1:26-27

Courtesy/Civility • Personal Life

21

Internet Pornography

There is a deadly cancer that is rapidly spreading in the church. Ironically, most leaders in the church know it exists, but we are not doing much to rid ourselves of this disease. It is causing family after family to become sick and fall away. This cancer goes by many names, but the most common name is internet pornography.

Within a single calendar year I counseled eight preachers who are struggling with this deadly temptation. The actual number of men (and women) struggling with this sin is staggering. On any given Sunday, in a congregation of 300, there are dozens of individuals fighting the battle of Internet porn.

The website *MBA Online*[1] recently did a thorough review of pornography usage in the United States, and uncovered that 12% of all Internet websites are pornography sites. In addition, 25% of all search engine requests are pornography related. A mind-numbing 2.5 billion pornographic emails are sent out each day!

In the past, pornography was sold "under the counter" with the purchaser having to walk into a store and leave with something normally wrapped in a brown paper bag. Today it is just one click or one swipe away. Not only is it easily accessible but consider as well the reality that most teens have access to the internet on their smart phones or tablets and you begin to see that this disease is only going to get worse - unless we address it in a serious "head-on" way!

Here's what I intend to teach my children on the topic of internet pornography.

Satan desperately wants you, and one of the ways in which he will likely try to tempt you is through the use of internet porn - images of naked people on the computer. I wish I could tell you that you will never have to worry about this issue but the reality is, this problem is epidemic. While your mom and dad do not currently struggle with this temptation, we are smart enough to know it is real, and as such, we have put filters on all of our computers in an effort to ward off the darts of Satan.

We recognize most porn addictions start with young people viewing pornography at age 11 or 12, so we are trying to protect your hearts and minds (Philippians 4:8). Let me begin by telling you that if you want your marriage to suffer and eventually crumble, then internet pornography is a sure-fire method to get you there. I have counseled many individuals who have gone from happy families just like ours, to having everything turned upside-down because of an obsession that is ruining their lives. Please don't open the door to this sin as it will lead to destruction.

Marriage is a wonderful thing. And it is within the confines of marriage that I hope one day you will experience the pleasure of an intimate relationship. Remember God instituted marriage, and it is good. But when you begin pursuing sexual pleasure outside the bounds of marriage

Flee sexual immorality. Every sin that a man does is outside the body, but he who commits sexual immorality sins against his own body.
~ 1 Corinthians 6:18

- even pleasure from a screen - you have crossed a line God did not intend for you to cross! You must therefore discipline yourself and not get started on a pathway to pornography (1 Corinthians 6:18). Part of being a New Testament Christian and walking in the light is learning how to control yourself and not give in to temptations (1 Thessalonians 4:3-5). I charge you to keep your eyes from anything wicked (Psalm 101:3).

Why?

First, those images are not images of your spouse, so what gives you the right to look at them? We are told to keep the marriage bed pure and undefiled before God (Hebrews 13:4).

Second, the person (male or female) in those naked images happens to be someone's child - a person created in the image of God. How would you feel if someone were lusting over your sister or brother in that fashion? You are to keep yourself unspotted from the world (James

Internet Pornography • Personal Life

23

1:27).

Third, viewing the images is causing you to lust for someone to whom you are not married (Matthew 5:27-28; Proverbs 6:20-35).

Fourth, many of those images will physically alter the pleasure center of your brain causing you to place unreal expectations on your spouse or future spouse - creating real problems in your marriage.

Fifth, those images reduce a beautiful experience God gave to married couples to a cheap perverted act. Finally, consider what it does to your spouse - the spouse who will discover your viewing habits after a while. How do you think it will make him or her feel?

If you ever feel yourself slipping into this world, please let me (or someone) know immediately. Get help. Find someone who can help you be accountable. Purchase filters for your computers. Share your passwords with your spouse so there is no hiding. And avoid "surfing" behavior that you know will lead you to viewing pornography. And if that doesn't work, then get rid of the computer all together. Put it to death (Colossians 3:5). Your soul and marriage are too valuable to lose over pornographic images (Galatians 6:8)!

For Discussion

IS PORNOGRAPHY ALWAYS VISUAL? CAN COMICS, OR GRAPHIC NOVELS BE CONSIDERED PORNOGRAPHY?

Verses for Further Study		
Philippians 4:8	Psalm 101:3	Proverbs 6:20-35
1 Corinthians 6:18	Hebrews 13:4	Colossians 3:5
1 Thessalonians 4:3-5	James 1:27	Galatians 6:8
	Matthew 5:27-28	

[1] http://www.onlinemba.com/blog/ stats-on-internet-pornography/

Prioritizing Your Time

I recently was having a conversation with a kind Christian mother who shared with me that her family was being pulled in to too many directions. She commented that she often felt overwhelmed, and felt like all she did as a parent was take her children from one activity to the next.

I asked the mom what all her family was involved in and she began to rattle off a long list: "Well, we have basketball practice two nights a week and then games on Saturday. Then, my oldest has band practice after school usually two days each week. My daughter wanted to play soccer this year, and so she's on a team that practices every Thursday and then games are either Monday evening or Saturday. We normally have 1-2 youth events each month, normally for each age group, and ... ." And on and on it went. I was tired just listening to this exhausted mom.

Sometimes my mouth engages before my brain and I find myself saying something that might not come out the way I intended.

I asked this Christian mother, "Just curiously, what activities are the kids involved in that don't center around themselves?"

She stopped, looked at me, and asked, "What do you mean?"

"Well, like visiting the sick, singing at the nursing home, visiting with shut-ins, visiting children's homes, helping with disaster relief, doing kind deeds for people who aren't expecting it" I replied.

She laughed and said, "You're kidding, right? I am already running nonstop. How could I squeeze even more activities into our hectic schedules?"

I wish this above scenario were an isolated event. But the reality is far too many Christian families are exhausting themselves by trying

25

Prioritizing Your Time • Personal Life

to take advantage of every opportunity the world has to offer. Parents feel guilty if their child is not signed up for several different sports or extracurricular activities each year. The bottom line is Satan has done a tremendous job keeping Christians busy in the secular world, to the neglect of our Christian duty — and our pulpits remain silent on it. After all, we don't want to cause any ripples and convict parents to alter their lifestyles.

Here's what I intend to teach my children regarding prioritizing your time.

I know what I'm about to tell you won't be popular with many. The Bible does not command you to play on a sports team or play in a band. It also does not command you to be involved in every extracurricular activity that comes down the pike. But it does speak clearly about things like visiting the sick, caring for the widows and orphans, and teaching those who are lost (Matthew 25:31-46; James 1:27; Matthew 28:16-20).

Now please hear what I am not saying. I am not saying those activities are in-and-of-themselves wrong. Your mom and I both enjoyed participating in some of those very things growing up. But the key is prioritizing your time — making sure that your Christian walk is not hindered by too many secular activities. In other words, your Christian life should never take a backseat.

Before you make the decision to become a Christian, you must count the cost (Luke 14:25-34). One of those "costs" is that you prioritize your time different from the world. However, I guarantee if you will prioritize your life the way God commands, your entire life will be richly blessed — far beyond anything a ball game could ever do.

Take a few minutes and think about how you spend your time. Where is the focus?

In James 1:27, we learn that pure religion is to care for orphans and look after widows. That's not just a verse that we memorize. It is a call to action. In Matthew 25:31-40, Jesus points out that it is those who feed the hungry, give the thirsty something to drink, welcome in strangers, give the naked clothing, and visit prisoners that will hear the words, "Come, you blessed of My Father, inherit the kingdom prepared for you from the foundation of the

Prioritizing Your Time • Personal Life

world" (vs. 34). Notice He never mentioned any of the activities that many young people are preoccupied with.

Your mom and I are trying to rear you to visit the sick and shut-ins. We have taken you to funerals since you were little so that you can "weep with those who weep" (Romans 12:15). As you know there have been occasions that we have said "No," to certain organized activities. That was not because we don't love you. But rather just the opposite. We love you so much that we don't want Satan disrupting our family life and our process of training you to be Christian warriors.

Take a few minutes and think about how you spend your time. Is it all focused on you or are you honestly seeking to do His will? Spend some time with the sick and shut-ins. While you are supposed to be making them feel better, it will be you who leaves feeling better for your time spent together. Remember, life is not all about you. It's all about Him.

Family Discussion

CALCULATE HOW MUCH TIME YOU SPEND ON SELF ENTERTAINMENT AS AN INDIVIDUAL, AND AS A FAMILY.

NOW CALCULATE HOW MUCH YOU SPEND IN HELPING OTHERS.

HOW CAN YOU CREATE A MORE CHRIST-LIKE BALANCE?

Verses for Further Study

| Matthew 25:31-46 | Matthew 28:16-20 | James 1:27 |
| James 1:27 | Luke 14:25-34 | Romans 12:15 |

Prioritizing Your Time • Personal Life

27

Shacking Up (Co-habitating)

Individuals — including Christians — are very reluctant to reassess their "traditional" worldview and admit they might have gotten some things wrong or fed a rise in immorality. Stop and consider for a moment the "traditional" view of college. A young person leaves home around age eighteen to run off and pursue higher education. If that were where things stopped, then it would be an admirable pursuit. But an honest evaluation demonstrates that as more and more people pursued that piece of parchment, there also was a shift in housing with a dramatic rise in unmarried people living together. Since 1960, the number of individuals cohabiting in the United States has increased fifteen-fold. Let that sink in for a moment.

Co-ed dorms used to be almost scandalous. Often it was brought on because of an imbalance in the percentage of males and females, and thus college administrations were forced to house both sexes together. Now, coed dorms are the norm at most universities — and they are sought out by many. In addition, many male and female students share apartments and houses to cut down on housing costs — all the while the moral belt for our society continues to be loosened.

But what about the church? Surely cohabitation is not affecting the church, right? Sadly, many Christians stood on the sidelines during the sexual revolution and allowed the world to teach our children a low view of marriage. As a result, more and more of our grown children began cohabitating — and it appears we, as a body of Christ followers, have forgotten how to blush.

Here's what I intend to teach my children regarding cohabitation.

It's not a big secret your mom and I were not big fans of lock-ins. We just could not see the good in it. We have strived to keep you pure and teach you the importance of remaining pure before God. At the same time we have tried to diligently impress upon you the magnitude and

28

importance of marriage — an institution that God, Himself, started (Genesis 2:23-24).

Some of the people you meet in the future will tell you that getting married is overated. Or they will say they don't want to get married because they don't want to get a divorce like their parents did. Or that a piece of paper is not all that important.

Please remember this: marriage matters.

It matters to God — and it needs to matter to you and your future mate. I hope that your reputation will be such that potential mates who are alright with co-habitating will not even bother coming around.

As you consider future living arrangements, I pray that you will always ask yourself what you are wanting from a relationship. Then search God's Word for the reasons given for marriage. Afterwards, weigh the eternal benefits of marriage versus living with someone. The Bible is clear that individuals who practice fornication (sexual relations outside of marriage) will not inherit the kingdom of Heaven (Galatians 5:19-21). The Bible says, "He who finds a wife finds a **good** thing, and obtains favor from the Lord" (Proverbs 18:22). It doesn't say "He who finds someone to sleep with and pay half the rent finds a good thing."

I could bore you with statistics about how those who cohabitate are less likely to stay together. Or I could share the facts about things like domestic violence, cheating, and chores — but I hope those numbers and facts aren't really necessary for you to understand the importance of this issue.

It is my prayer that your mother and I have burned your conscience in such a way that the very thought of "shacking up" with someone makes you uncomfortable and causes you to blush. Go back and study passages like Hebrews 13:4; 1 Corinthians 6:18-20; 1 Corinthians 7:2; Revelation 21:8; and 2 Timothy 2:22. While others may not be worried about their earthly reputation I hope you will be — for you serve and represent the God who instituted marriage!

Verses for Further Study

Genesis 2:23-24	Hebrews 13:4	1 Corinthians 7:2
Galatians 5:19-21	1 Corinthians 6:18-20	Revelation 21:8
Proverbs 18:22		2 Timothy 2:22

Shacking Up (Co-habitating) • Personal Life

Relationships

Relationships are a normal part of life. The Bible says, "For none of us lives to himself, and no one dies to himself" (Romans 14:7). In other words, it is impossible to live a life that is unaffected by other people.

Humans were created to be social beings. We came from a God that is a part of the Godhead (which demonstrates unity), who sent His Son to earth for each of us, and we are added to a church full of individuals we are called to rejoice and weep with (Romans 12:15). Look at the example set by the first century church:

> Now all who believed were together, and had all things in common, and sold their possessions and goods, and divided them among all, as anyone had need. So continuing daily with one accord in the temple, and breaking bread from house to house, they ate their food with gladness and simplicity of heart (Acts 2:44-46).

Sadly, many people seek their identity through relationships. In other words, these individuals look for meaning, purpose, a sense of well-being, and even approval from their relationships with other people. Consider what happens when this relationship experiences troubles (which happens in most relationships), or if the relationship ends.

Here's what I intend to teach my children regarding relationships.

The book of Proverbs warns us of some things of which to beware. It describes a number of foolish behaviors we would do well to avoid in relationships when we see it in others: gossip and division (Proverbs 16:28); anger and violence (Proverbs 16:29); lying (Proverbs 12:22); greed (Proverbs 15:27); and lack of compassion (Proverbs 29:7).

In writing to the church at Corinth, Paul admonished, "But now I have written to you not to keep company with anyone named a brother, who is sexually immoral, or covetous, or an idolater, or a reviler, or a drunkard, or an extortioner—not even to eat with such a person" (1 Corinthians 5:11). Paul outlines for us just how important relationships and influence are for Christians. Over and over, the Bible tells us to be on the lookout for "wolves in sheep's clothing." (See 2 Thessalonians 2:3; 2 Peter 3:17; 1 John 4:1.) Why is this a big deal when it comes to forming relationships, and how does it pertain to you personally? Ask yourself if it is possible that you have allowed some wolves into your circle of friends.

As you reflect on those you associate with, ask yourself: What are some unrealistic expectations people have about relationships? Then spend a minute reflecting on what are some of the best qualities you bring to a relationship.

The Bible is full of examples of good relationships. Consider for example: David and Jonathan, Naomi and Ruth, Jesus and His disciples, etc. Likewise, there are many examples of bad relationships in the Bible: Cain and Abel, Paul and Barnabas, Jesus and Judas, etc. Let me encourage you to study these relationships and learn from them.

Good *Biblical Relationships*

David & Jonathan
Naomi & Ruth
Jesus & His disciples

Bad *Biblical Relationships*

Cain & Abel
Paul & Barnabas
Jesus & Judas

As you build relationships with those around you, make sure those relationships don't become more about your own little kingdoms rather than the kingdom of God. Unfortunately, many people build relationships based on what they want out of their lives rather than what God wants for our lives. While these selfish relationships may feed a part of you for a short period of time, they will ultimately implode. Consider for a moment what happens when you get into a relationship expecting something, but God produces a different result than what you were expecting? Get into a relationship based on wanting to please God first—not yourself!

As you read through Scripture, ask yourself what are some signs of a healthy relationship? Likewise, what are some signs of an unhealthy relationship? Paul wrote to the church at Corinth that *"evil company corrupts good habits"* (1 Corinthians 15:33). His words are still very

Relationships • Personal Life

31

applicable today.

The reality is you have surrounded yourself with people who are either going to be influenced by you or who are going to influence you. These influences can either be positive and draw you closer to God, or they can be negative and pull you away from Him. Learn how to identify negative influences and limit those in your life.

The way in which you build relationships with others will eventually affect who you marry and how you rear your children. It is my prayer that you will build healthy relationships now, so that as you begin looking for a mate for life, you already have the tools necessary to get into a healthy marriage relationship!

Family Discussion

HOW MUCH ENERGY SHOULD YOU PUT INTO IMPROVING A TOXIC RELATIONSHIP?

IS IT WRONG TO AVOID ALL CONTACT WITH SOMEONE?

HOW CAN YOU IMPROVE THE RELATIONSHIPS IN YOUR LIFE?

Verses for Further Study

Romans 14:7	Proverbs 12:22	2 Thessalonians 2:3
Romans 12:15	Proverbs 15:27	2 Peter 3:17
Acts 2:44-46	Proverbs 29:7	1 John 4:1
Proverbs 16:28	1 Corinthians 5:11	1 Corinthians 15:33

Relationships • Personal Life

32

Verbal Abuse

There are thousands of children who are reared in homes where a parent never strikes another parent, and yet, these children are eyewitnesses to abuse. Verbal abuse is real and it hurts. Some think verbal abuse isn't really abusive since there are no bruises left behind. However, the scars from verbal abuse run deep. Words can cut deep.

Verbal abuse is one of those "elephants in the room." Those who use it often have an entire arsenal at their disposal to tear someone else down. We all know it occurs, and may have even witnessed a minor case of it between husband and wife (or between parent and child or between boyfriend and girlfriend), but it's one of those topics that makes us uncomfortable and rarely gets addressed from the pulpit. Without blood and bruises, this sin gets washed away as no big deal— and as a result marriages crumble and lives are changed forever. However, verbal abuse is a sin, and it is often a sin that goes on for decades unless someone is confronted and truly repents.

Here's what I intend to teach my children regarding verbal abuse.

You have never seen me hit your mother in any fashion other than an occasional love pat. And you never will! I grew up learning real men do not hit women — ever. That is a lesson that should become a permanent part of our family legacy: Harrub men do not hit their wives. (And likewise, Harrub ladies don't hit their husbands!) Period!

1 Peter 3:7 admonishes, "Husbands, likewise, dwell with them with understanding, giving honor to the wife, as to the weaker vessel, and as being heirs together of the grace of life, that your prayers may not be hindered." Your mom is the weaker vessel—and rather than take advantage of that and be domineering, I should love, treasure, and give honor to her. Now I realize there are women out there stronger than me, some much stronger, but as a general statement, men are stronger than women. Just because you are bigger does not give you the right to

33

push anyone else around, especially your spouse!

But that's not our true topic of discussion today. Today I want to teach you about another type of abuse that can be just as harmful, and that is verbal abuse. When I was little, there was a saying: "Sticks and stones can break my bones, but words can never hurt me." Parents would teach this to their children who might be getting bullied on a playground. While the saying sounded good at the time, the truth is that words hurt. The proverb writer described it "like the piercings of a sword" (Proverbs 12:18).

But the tongue of the wise **promotes** health. A child that is called "fat" or "retarded" during childhood may carry that pain for decades. Words have power. The Bible says, "Death and life are in the power of the tongue, and those who love it will eat its fruit" (Proverbs 18:21).

Let me first remind you that you will be held accountable for your words. In talking to the Pharisees, Jesus rebuked them saying, "But I say to you that for every idle word men may speak, they will give account of it in the day of judgment. For by your words you will be justified, and by your words you will be condemned" (Matthew 12:36-37).

Sticks and stones can break bones, and words DO hurt!

Previously, I have reminded you that a husband is to love his wife like Christ loves the church (Ephesians 5:25). Jesus would never verbally abuse His bride, the church. Paul wrote, "Let no corrupt word proceed out of your mouth, but what is good for necessary edification, that it may impart grace to the hearers" (Ephesians 4:29).

James reminds us:

And the tongue is a fire, a world of iniquity. The tongue is so set among our members that it defiles the whole body, and sets on fire the course of nature; and it is set on fire by hell. For every kind of beast and bird, of reptile and creature of the sea, is tamed and has been tamed by mankind. But no man can tame the tongue. It is an unruly evil, full of deadly poison. With it we bless our God and Father, and with it we curse men, who have been made in the similitude of God (James 3:6-9).

Jesus pointed out the seriousness of the tongue in His famous

Verbal Abuse • Personal Life

"Sermon on the Mount". In that lesson, He noted, "You have heard that it was said to those of old, 'You shall not murder, and whoever murders will be in danger of the judgment.' But I say to you that whoever is angry with his brother without a cause shall be in danger of the judgment. And whoever says to his brother, 'Raca!' shall be in danger of the council. But whoever says, 'You fool!' shall be in danger of hell fire" (Matthew 5:21-22).

If you find yourself yelling at someone, or cutting them down, or hurting them with your words, it indicates a deeper problem. Jesus observed, "A good man out of the good treasure of his heart brings forth good; and an evil man out of the evil treasure of his heart brings forth evil. For out of the abundance of the heart his mouth speaks" (Luke 6:45). If you are verbally abusing someone, it says something about your own heart.

God gave you a mouth — use it for building up, not tearing down (1 Thessalonians 5:11). Because just as Harrub men don't hit their wives, Harrub men also don't hit their wives with cruel words!

Family Discussion

WHY DO WORDS MATTER SO MUCH?

HOW CAN YOU STAND UP FOR THE RIGHT WHEN YOU WITNESS VERBAL ABUSE OF SOMEONE ELSE?

Verses for Further Study

1 Peter 3:7	Ephesians 4:29
Proverbs 12:18	James 3:6-9
Proverbs 18:21	Matthew 5:21-22
Matthew 12:36-37	Luke 6:45
Ephesians 5:25	1 Thess 5:11

Verbal Abuse • Personal Life

Getting Your Feelings Hurt

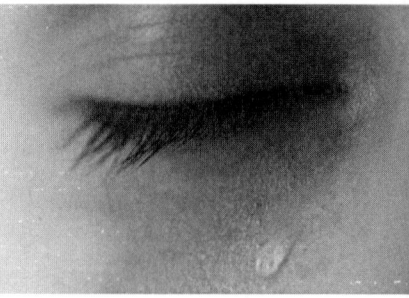

It happens to any human that lives to be the age of ten. Sooner or later someone is going to hurt your feelings. Maybe they make fun of something you are wearing. Or a group of friends goes out to eat together and you are left out. Or maybe the attacks are much worse. Maybe someone attacks your character or says something about you that is not true. How do we deal with this? What is our normal recourse of action?

The honest truth is that Christians do not handle conflict very well. Too often we either do nothing at all, trying to avoid any form of conflict, or our emotions propel us to overreact. Isn't it interesting that the church is made up of individuals—many of whom have trouble getting along—and yet our pulpits often remain silent about what to do when you get your feelings hurt? I think many of the "problems" we have in the church today could be fixed or avoided if we would just spend some time discussing hurt feelings.

Here's what I intend to teach my children regarding getting their feelings hurt.

You will get your feelings hurt. In fact, I've probably already been one of the ones to hurt your feelings. Congratulations—welcome to the human race. This is one of those things that you will deal with the rest of your life, because people are not perfect.

The first thing I want you to do the next time you get your feelings hurt is to stop and ask yourself if you are really all that important. Part of the reason our feelings are hurt is because someone offended us— which means we probably have a pretty high view of ourselves. "How dare them do that to me?!" Or, "How dare them say that about me?!" Before you ask questions like that, check yourself—and remind yourself that you are not God or His sinless Son. In fact, what you are is a sinner in need of a spotless sacrifice. Don't forget that.

Second, do your best to treat the offending person the way you would want to be treated. In Matthew 7:12, Jesus commanded, "Therefore, whatever you want men to do to you, do also to them, for this is the Law and the Prophets." This is a tough one, because if you feel hurt, your normal tendency may be to lash out or punish the offender. Treat them how you would want to be treated. Because the reality is you may not know the entire situation. How many times are people wrestling with things (e.g., sickness, death of a loved one, stress at work, etc.) and you have little to no knowledge of it. Yes, they may have hurt your feelings — but you may just be receiving bitterness due to something that is more troubling in their life. It doesn't excuse their behavior, but hopefully you might be able to better understand and be more compassionate.

Third, follow Biblical principles. The Bible has advice to both those who are offended and those who offend. In Matthew 18:15, Jesus admonishes, "Moreover if your brother sins against you, go and tell him his fault between you and him alone. If he hears you, you have gained your brother." So, have the courage to talk to them. Likewise, in Matthew 5:23-24, we read, "Therefore if you bring your gift to the altar, and there remember that your brother has something against you, leave your gift there before the altar, and go your way. First be reconciled to your brother, and then come and offer your gift." Sadly, when someone hurts us, we expect them to do what Scripture says and come to us, but rarely do we go to them as Jesus recorded in Matthew 18. Both parties have a responsibility. Part of the reason I wanted you to first ask yourself if you were that important is to check your pride. Pride has stopped more relationships from healing than probably any other issue. Swallow your pride and talk to the person. You might be surprised at how quickly something can be cleared up when you just sit down and talk.

Lastly, remember these are just your feelings. The Bible records in Jeremiah 17:19, "The heart is deceitful above all things, and desperately wicked; Who can know it?" Some people want to "speak their mind" when their feelings get hurt. However, what you should be doing is speaking the mind of Christ. At the end of the day, God is what matters. Do not allow your hurt feelings to slow you down from your ultimate purpose. Satan would love for Christians to be caught up in petty feuds over hurt feelings. This one is a tough one—and you will have to constantly be working on it. Just remember, when you lay your head on your pillow that even if all your friends make fun of you, there is still a God in heaven who loves you!

Verses for Further Study

Matthew 5:23-24; 7:12; 18   Jeremiah 17:19

Getting Your Feelings Hurt • Personal Life

Chivalry

Try this experiment: Stand in a parking lot near the entrance to a building and watch how young men treat those around them. Car doors are rarely opened for ladies. Entrance doors are often opened just long enough for the young men to get through, slamming shut in the face of others. Rarely will you see someone exhibit a code of conduct that is purposefully thinking of others. Our society is so self-absorbed that rarely do we see small acts of kindness.

A mixture of radical feminism and an unhealthy dose of selfishness slammed the door shut on the most basic of chivalrous deeds. Even within the church, our behavior has been influenced. Far too often, individuals think only of themselves — focusing on their needs instead of the needs of others.

Here is what I intend to teach my children about chivalry.

In the wee hours of the night on April 19, 1912, the *R.M.S. Titanic* struck an iceberg and began to quickly sink. As lifeboats were lowered into the water the call rang out, "Women and children first!" The men onboard lived by a code, and that code of life declared that the women should be protected and cared for. A recent high school survey asked teenage boys if they would do the same if they were in that position, and many of the young men laughed at the very thought. Our attitudes have changed a lot in the last 100 years.

This notion of taking care of ladies, weaker individuals, widows, or orphans was once the virtue of knights in what became known as chivalry. Wikipedia indicates the term chivalry was derived "from the French term chevalerie, meaning horse soldiery — and it involves honor, gallantry, and individual training and service to others. Over time its meaning has been refined to emphasize more ideals such as knightly virtues, honor, courtly love, courtesy, and less martial aspects

38

of the tradition. *The Knight's Code of Chivalry* was a moral system that stated all knights should protect others who can not protect themselves, such as widows, children, and elders."

If that last part sounds familiar, it is because James used it to describe pure religion. "Pure and undefiled religion before God and the Father is this: to visit orphans and widows in their trouble, and to keep oneself unspotted from the world" (James 1:27). Some would argue that chivalry is dead. I would contend that as long as there are Christians around to carry out James' definition of pure religion then chivalry will be alive and well. Being kind will never go out of style in the sight of God.

Let me encourage you to get into the habit of opening doors, helping someone with their coat, lending an arm to someone who is unsteady, offering an umbrella when it rains, protecting those who are weak, etc. This will become good practice for when you are married. In 1 Peter 3:7 we read, "Husbands, likewise, dwell with them with understanding, **giving honor to the wife, as to the weaker vessel**, and as being heirs together of the grace of life, that your prayers may not be hindered" (emp. added). Notice it says weaker vessel but not unequal! Males and females are equal in the sight of God.

I'm pretty sure I still have sore places where I was unexpectedly struck by a sword when you were little pretending to be a knight. I cherish those memories — on occasion you would fiercely protect your sister, and on others she would receive the brunt of your sword as you captured her and took her to your secret hiding place. What you did not know back then was most true knights lived by an ancient code of chivalry.

> *Chivalry is about protecting those who can not protect themselves.*

Look over this list from Wikipedia:
The code can be summarized in 11 "commandments:"
- Believe the church's teachings and observe all the Church's directions.
- Defend the church.
- Respect and defend all weaknesses.
- Love your country.
- Do not recoil before an enemy.

• A single coward could discourage an entire army. Even if the knights knew death was near, they would rather die fighting than show weakness.
• Show no mercy to the infidel. Do not hesitate to make war with them.
• Perform all duties that agree with the laws of God.
• Never lie or go back on one's word.
• Be generous to everyone.
• Always and everywhere be right and good against evil and injustice.

While we don't follow every single one of those today, you can see that these men truly did care for the weak and tried to do right. Don't give up your sword — the world needs more knights!

Consider what the world would be like if we all treated each other with kindness, thinking of others. I want to encourage you to keep chivalry alive in your heart. Never forget the words of Jesus when He said, "And just as you want men to do to you, you also do to them likewise" (Luke 6:31).

Family Activity

CREATE A KNIGHT'S CODE FOR YOUR HOUSEHOLD, THEN POST IT IN A PROMINANT PLACE.

Verses for Further Study

James 1:27	1 Peter 3:7	Luke 6:31

Vanity

There have been many articles and sermons preached about how Christians dress for Sunday morning worship. A visiting alien might assume that one of the biggest problems facing Christendom today is casual attire in the assembly. Let me clarify that I do believe one should look good when worshipping our Creator—and I don't like the trend toward sloppy casual dress.

However, having said that, I believe there is another side of the coin that many faithful Christians overlook—probably because it is a struggle in which they inwardly struggle. (Sometimes we find it easier to point out the speck rather than focusing on the log in our own eyes.) The truth of the matter is many people struggle with vanity. We want our clothes to fit just right. We want our hair to lay just right. We want to wear the right name brands and latest styles.

In this age of "Selfies" and cosmetic surgery, many Christians have fallen prey to vanity. It's all about "the look" rather than "the God." Even preachers and elders have fallen victim to caring about what people think and padding their resumes with accomplishments to impress others. Many are more worried about posturing than they are their own relationship with Christ. The reality is too many people are worried about their outward appearance.

Here's what I intend on teaching my children about vanity.

Your mom and I have often talked about how much better the world would be without mirrors. Think about that for just a moment—a world where you couldn't constantly see what you looked like. How much time do you think the average person spends on their appearance each day? Now ask yourself this important question: How much time do these individuals spend each day making sure his/her heart and personality "look" good?

This topic you will probably find difficult, as our culture is telling

41

you the opposite of what the Bible says. Vanity is defined in the dictionary as "excessive pride in one's appearance or accomplishments; conceit." This is not the description of a bondservant of Christ. When Claire was little, we wrote Proverbs 31:30 on her wall as a reminder of what is truly important, "Charm is deceitful and beauty is passing, But a woman who fears the Lord, she shall be praised."

Study the following verses:

• "Turn away my eyes from looking at worthless things, And revive me in Your way" (Psalms 119:37).
• But the Lord said to Samuel, "Do not look at his appearance or at his physical stature, because I have refused him. For the Lord does not see as man sees; for man looks at the outward appearance, but the Lord looks at the heart" (1 Samuel 16:7).
• "Though you clothe yourself with crimson, Though you adorn yourself with ornaments of gold, Though you enlarge your eyes with paint, In vain you will make yourself fair" (Jeremiah 4:30).
• "Take heed that you do not do your charitable deeds before men, to be seen by them. Otherwise you have no reward from your Father in heaven" (Matthew 6:1).

Looking nice and having a good appearance is a balance. Yes, we want your hair brushed when you go to church. We also want you to bathe (and use soap!) on a regular occasion. But my prayer is that you will not place too much emphasis on your outward appearance. Work more on your inward appearance—for if it is beautiful it will radiate out in such a way that your true beauty will shine. If you find yourself looking at a mirror often, ask yourself why.

Be comfortable in your outward appearance, because after all God created you that way. And if you find yourself surrounded by those who are overly concerned with looks, you might ask yourself if these individuals are truly putting first things first?! This one will take some effort—because as I said our culture is working hard to get you to obsess with your outward appearance. Don't give in. Be transformed and renew your mind.

Verses for Further Study

| Proverbs 31:30 | 1 Samuel 16:7 | Matthew 6:1 |
| Psalms 119:37 | Jeremiah 4:30 | |

Longsuffering

One of the costs of living in a technologically advanced world is the constant urgency we place on everything. Regular "snail mail" shipping is no longer good enough—we order something online and we want it instantly (or at least within 48 hours)! Our society has become impatient as we hustle and bustle about in our daily walks.

But all of this rushing about and technological advances have resulted, in many cases, in weakened personal relationships. Simply put we don't have time for people anymore—and when we do interact, often, it is in a negative fashion. We are quick to get angry and in many cases self-restraint has been thrown to the wind. People are quick to point out the negative in others or unleash anger on someone who didn't live up to expectations. Sadly, our country seems content to rear a generation of self-absorbed individualists rather than to heal a broken nation.

In a day in which a Facebook post can instantly dissolve friendships, and intolerance of Biblical convictions seems to be the rule rather than the exception, the world is in desperate need of longsuffering. It is a word that is not used often, but is frequently mentioned in the Bible. It is one of those words we hear occasionally, but don't hear too many lessons on.

Here is what I intend to teach my children about longsuffering.

Part of our goal in life is to become less like the world and more and more like God as we draw closer to Him. One of the characteristics of God found in both the Old Testament and New Testament is longsuffering (e.g., Exodus 34:6; Numbers 14:18; Psalms 86:15; Romans 2:4; 9:22; 2 Corinthians 6:6; Colossians 1:11; 1 Peter 3:20; 2 Peter 3:15). When you were young, you memorized the "fruits of the Spirit," and it is no mistake that long-suffering is included in that list (Galatians 5:22-23). But what does this word really mean?

The actual Greek word is *makrothumia. Makro* is commonly

43

translated "long" and *thumos* is translated "temper." It is literally the opposite of short-tempered. This quality defines someone who is not quick to anger and uses self-restraint. The apostle Paul instructed the Christians at Colossae, "Therefore, as the elect of God, holy and beloved, put on tender mercies, kindness, humility, meekness, longsuffering;" (Colossians 3:12). He also mentioned this quality to the Christians at Ephesus, "with all lowliness and gentleness, with longsuffering, bearing with one another in love," Ephesians 4:2. In fact, this trait is so important that Paul informed young Timothy that Jesus Christ had shown a pattern of longsuffering for us to follow (1 Timothy 1:16).

Longsuffering is a character trait that must be developed—and should not be dependent on how someone else treats you. Consider God's longsuffering of mankind. It requires persistence and a desire to be more pleasing to God. This is one of those traits that your dad still has to work on, even as an adult—but I can tell you it does get easier with time.

There will be many occasions in your life where disagreements come up. How you deal with those disagreements is a reflection of you and tells a person how well you practice this godly trait of longsuffering. 1 Corinthians 13 reminds us that longsuffering is "love" on trial. While getting angry and shouting may make your point, it also says a lot about you as a person—and whether you are cultivating the fruits of the Spirit. Are you thinking more about self, or treating others as you would have them treat you (Matthew 7:12)?

It won't take you long in life to realize there are many people who you will disagree with over various subjects. How do you think God would have you react in these situations? Before you respond in haste, remind yourself how you would feel if every time you made a mistake God quickly rebuked you. Practice longsuffering and you will quickly discover that the ability to demonstrate self-restraint will be beneficial in all walks of life—work, church, and family. At the end of the day, remember it's not about rushing here and there and having things your way—but rather it's about the souls of men.

Verses for Further Study

Exodus 34:6	2 Corinthians 6:6	Galatians 5:22-23
Numbers 14:18	Colossians 1:11; 3:12	Ephesians 4:2
Psalms 86:15	1 Peter 3:20	1 Timothy 1:16
Romans 2:4; 9:22	2 Peter 3:15	Matthew 7:12

Lust

In a hyper-sexualized nation we have almost become desensitized to it: lust. Scantily clad billboards are the norm. Restaurants featuring immodestly dressed women are not just doing well—they are thriving and new chains, also featuring immodest waitresses, are sprouting up in cities all across the nation. Television has become a parade of indecently dressed actors and actresses. Even many commercials use sex to sell products and feature immodest actresses.

Many people are dressing not just to attract attention, but to also accentuate their bodies. Our society feels very comfortable wearing very little or very tight clothes. A Christian would be hard pressed to go to a local mall and not feel visually assaulted. Add to this the epidemic of Internet pornography and you can easily see the recipe for disaster. Infidelity has become the norm in television sitcoms, and marriages are falling apart all across the nation. And if we are honest with ourselves, lust does not stop at the doorway of a church building.

Here's what I intend to teach my children regarding lust.

God created our bodies—and He created them "good." The human body is an amazing thing. Unfortunately, many people have taken the human body and turned it into an ungodly object.

A simple definition of lust is longing for someone to whom you are not married. Lust is not something that Christians should be doing. Jesus said, "But I say to you that whoever looks at a woman to lust for her has already committed adultery with her in his heart" (Matthew 5:28). I believe part of the reason Christ said this was because the act of lusting removes the "human" element that was created in the image and likeness of God, and reduces that person down to an object. It also causes your mind to turn away from good things and to focus on fleshly things. In that moment you are walking away from a holy God.

Your mom and I have tried hard to shelter you from much of this

Lust • Christian Character

45

filth during your short lifetimes—and we encourage you to do the same in your homes. We know you are exposed to many sexual images when we go out in public, but we do everything we can to limit that exposure and to protect your hearts and minds. Many people would argue that children should not be sheltered because they claim that protective "bubble" is not what the real world is like. However, God does not (and does not need to) immerse His children in vile and graphic details so that you can "learn" and recognize sin. You do not need to experience sin to know what it is (e.g., Jesus did not need to experience sin to know what was sinful). We have reared you in such a way that hopefully you will not even open your minds to the sin of lust.

Many people lust because they view it to be a "secret sin" that no one else is aware of. However, God is aware of everything—and please remember that what you are doing is bringing your mind into darkness instead of the light. The writer of Proverbs instructed his son to keep his father's command, "To keep you from the evil woman, from the flattering tongue of a seductress. Do not lust after her beauty in your heart" (Proverbs 6:24-25). Later in that same book we read, "The righteousness of the upright will deliver them, but the unfaithful will be caught by their lust" (Proverbs 11:6).

Lust is a battle of the mind. What you must do is constantly discipline your mind against going there. Paul in writing to the church at Galatia admonished, "I say then: Walk in the Spirit, and you shall not fulfill the lust of the flesh. For the flesh lusts against the Spirit, and the Spirit against the flesh; and these are contrary to one another, so that you do not do the things that you wish" (Galatians 5:16-17). Every time you find yourself in that battle, consider that it was our wretched sin that put Jesus Christ on the cross. Force yourself to consider the real cost of making someone into an object for your pleasure. The cost of sin is death—it's not worth a few minutes of mental pleasure.

Verses for Further Study

Matthew 5:28	Proverbs 11:6
Proverbs 6:24-25	Galatians 5:16-17

Boldness

For many children, it is a weekly observation—they hear Mom and Dad profess a love and allegiance to God, but that love is rarely expressed outside the home or church building. Seldom do we talk to non-Christians about our faith or love of Christ. Rarely do we confront sin or share with strangers the "Good News." Yes, we say we are Christians, but often our actions display a group of people who has grown apathetic and timid.

Rare is the pulpit that will stir Christians' hearts toward getting out among the lost. Oh sure, we talk about it in general terms—but we don't mention street names in our neighborhoods. Instead of risking disfavor and encouraging Christians to get out of their "comfort zones," preachers and elders will often play it safe and feed this fearful mindset with undemanding messages. As a result, Christians today grow lethargic, and the Gospel is rarely shared.

Here's what I intend to teach my children about being bold.

There are going to be times you find yourself feeling uncomfortable. There may even be people who slam a door, hang up a phone, or block you on social media. But, as your mom often says: "They can't take away your birthday or salvation!" Just remember that whatever you endure pales in comparison to what Christ went through. Instead of walking away sad or embarrassed, remember the words of James: "My brethren, count it all joy when you fall into various trials, knowing that the testing of your faith produces patience" (James 1:2-3).

In His famous Sermon on the Mount, Jesus declared, "Blessed are you when they revile and persecute you, and say all kinds of evil against you falsely for My sake. Rejoice and be exceedingly glad, for great is your reward in heaven, for so they persecuted the prophets who were before you" (Matthew 5:11-12).

My prayer is that you will be bold for Him! It has gotten so common

Boldness • Christian Character

47

for people not to talk openly about their faith or salvation that it almost feels weird when someone does it. Let me encourage you—be weird! Talk to people about Jesus Christ. Ask people questions about their salvation or their belief in God. Yes, you may occasionally find individuals who are turned off by it—but you will also be amazed by the number of people who want to talk about their faith or have questions about God! You will never find these individuals if you do not have the courage to speak up.

I love the picture painted for us in the early chapters of Acts. Peter was boldly preaching that the people needed to repent and be converted (Acts 3:19). Because of their boldness, Peter and John were arrested (Acts 4:3). When they were brought before the rulers and elders, Peter again pointed out that they had crucified Jesus Christ (Acts 4:10) and that "Nor is there salvation in any other, for there is no other name under heaven given among men by which we must be saved" (Acts 4:12). The response? The rulers and elders severely threatened them that they should not speak the name of Jesus. "So they called them and commanded them not to speak at all nor teach in the name of Jesus" (Acts 4:18). Peter and John continued to preach. In fact, rather than cowering down and becoming comfortable these men prayed, "Now, Lord, look on their threats, and grant to Your servants that with all boldness they may speak Your word" (Acts 4:29). In Acts 5:17-18, we find the Apostles being put in prison once again. An angel of the Lord comes to them that night and commands them to go back out and speak the "words of this life" (Acts 5:20).

So, by this point, these men have been threatened (repeatedly) and imprisoned. Yet what did they do? Early the next morning, they were teaching again in the temple (Acts 5:21). My prayer is that you will have this kind of boldness during your lifetime. Be like those bopping punching bags we had when I was little—get knocked down and just pop right back up! Yes, you may occasionally find yourself tired or discouraged, but never forget why you are doing what you are doing—and don't forget who you serve. "Have I not commanded you? Be strong and of good courage; do not be afraid, nor be dismayed, for the Lord your God is with you wherever you go" (Joshua 1:9)

Verses for Further Study

James 1:2-3	Acts 4:10	Acts 5:17-18
Matthew 5:11-12	Acts 4:12	Acts 5:20,21
Acts 3:19	Acts 4:18	Joshua 1:9
Acts 4:3	Acts 4:29	

Boldness • Christian Character

Obedience

The church buildings and religious programming on Sunday morning do not paint the accurate picture. If one were to drive around many cities in North America, you might believe that our society has embraced God and that Christianity is in good shape in our country (especially in the southern "Bible Belt" where you can see church buildings on most corners!). But the truth holds a far different picture. The reality is that while individuals may attend a worship service on Sunday, we live in a land of increasing immorality and corruptness. Approximately two thousand years ago Jesus observed

> You hypocrites! Well did Isaiah prophesy of you, when he said: "This people honor me with their lips, but their heart is far from me; in vain do they worship me, teaching as doctrines the commandments of men." (Matthew 15:7-9)

The reality is we don't mind God - and even relish the thought of Heaven - but many inwardly recoil at the thought of being obedient to Him. Many blame this rebellion against authority on the "anti-establishment" period in the "1960s-70s. But the reality is man has viewed obedience as a curse for much longer.

Here's what I intend to teach my children regarding obedience.

The one virtue God required of Adam was obedience. Think about that for a moment. All Adam did was eat a fruit, and for that sin of disobedience the entire world was forever changed. Men have struggled with obedience from the time of the Garden. Obedience is a central theme all throughout God's Word. Jesus Christ - our Master teacher - spent His entire time on earth in complete obedience to His heavenly Father. Our constant question as a Christian should be, "How can I obey and please God perfectly?"

49

Obedience • Christian Character

Let me make sure you understand that you cannot work your way into Heaven - Christ was the spotless sacrifice needed, and you can add nothing to that You are saved by grace and the blood of Jesus Christ! However, the knowledge of your redemption should penetrate your heart in such a way that you want to change (repentance) and want to become more Christlike. In short, your love for God should cause you to want to obey Him! (After all, His commands are for our good.)

As we study God's Word, we find obedience begins in Paradise, the Garden of Eden (Genesis 2:16) and runs all the way to the end of the Bible (Revelation 22:14). It should not be missed that in the Garden of

> *L et me make sure you understand - you cannot work your way into Heaven.*

Eden obedience to God's command "is the one virtue of Paradise." Obedience was the single thing that covered Adam and Eve. Paul, in his letter to the Christians at Rome observed, "For as by one man's disobedience many were made sinners, so also by one man's obedience many will be made righteous" (Romans 5:19).

In 1 Samuel 15:22-23, we find Samuel declaring to Saul, "To obey is better than sacrifice . . Because you have rejected the word of the Lord, He also has rejected you " Consider the strong words found in Jeremiah, "For I did not speak to your fathers, or command them in the day that I brought them out of the land of Egypt, concerning burnt offerings or sacrifices. But this is what I commanded them, saying, 'Obey My voice, and I will be your God, and you shall be My people'" (Jeremiah 7 22-23).

All throughout the Bible we find examples of obedience, such as Noah who obeyed what God commanded (Genesis 6:22; 7:5, 9, 16). Likewise, "by faith Abraham obeyed" (Hebrews 11: 8), To Moses at Mt Sinai, God declared, "If you will indeed obey My voice and keep My covenant, then you shall be a special treasure to Me above all people" (Exodus 19:5). The concept of obedience is all throughout Scripture. If it is all throughout Scripture, it should be all throughout you as well.

By studying the Scriptures we are able to discern, in a small way, the mind of God. One of the secrets to obedience, is having a personal relationship to God. It is that personal relationship that keeps His commands ever-present in our minds and keeps us from disobeying

Him. But this is a learning process that will last much of your lifetime. In the "classroom" of obedience Jesus acts as our teacher, the Bible is our textbook, and we are the students. Jesus admonished, "Why do you call me ' Lord, Lord,' and not do what I tell you?" (Luke 6:46).

Please don't forget that obedience should include Jesus' last commands to "Go" into all the world - the great commission. If we are truly going to live obedient lives to God then part of that must be telling others about Him. Our desire should not be to obey because of legalistic requirements, but rather to obey the loving Lord who promises each one of us eternal life. It is my prayer you will grow up with the words of the psalmist on your lips: "I delight to do Your will, O my God, and Your law is within my heart." (Psalm 40:8)

Family Discussion

HOW IMPORTANT IS OUR ATTITUDE WHEN
IT COMES TO OBEDIENCE?

Verses for Further Study

Matthew 15:7-9	1 Samuel 15:22-23	Hebrews 11: 8
Genesis 2:16	Jeremiah 7 22-23	Exodus 19:5
Revelation 22:14	Genesis 6:22; 7:5,	Luke 6:46
Romans 5:19	9, 16	Psalm 40:8

Obedience • Christian Character

Finishing the Course

We often don't do the best job of celebrating true success within the church. Oh, we celebrate births, bigger buildings, and even special days (e.g., Friends and Family day); but our young people don't see us celebrating true success—that is an elderly person who has remained faithful into the twilight years of his or her life.

What a beautiful sight to see someone who has been a faithful Christian for sixty years, who still remains active—doing what he or she can, right up to the point they step out into eternity. Our children need to comprehend that true success is not found in a fancy car or a big house in a wealthy neighborhood, but rather a complete life lived for Him.

Here is what I intend on telling my children about perseverance and running the race.

There is nothing like the feeling of coming up out of the water after being baptized. There is a freshness and zeal that is indescribable. I enjoy being around new Christians and listening to their passion. It is quite palpable in those who recognize that their sins have been washed away. But all too often that passion and zeal begins to wane. Revelation 2:4 calls it leaving your "first love."

I pray that you will finish your Christian life with the same passion and zeal with which you begin. The natural order of things indicates I will die without seeing this through, but I beg you to begin your Christian life with the end in mind. Focus on finishing strong. In fact, you know I've never been one to set the bar low, so my hope is that you will finish your life with even more passion and more zeal as you enter the twilight years of your life.

I can't tell you how many people I've watched who were on fire for the Lord for months, years, or even decades—and then threw it all away. Some have told me they got "burned out," while others have

52

simply become choked out by the cares of the world (Luke 8:14). These are individuals who came to a full knowledge of the Truth, but turned back, similar to what we read about in John 6:66, "From that time many of His disciples went back and walked with Him no more."

Will there be days or weeks where you are tired? Absolutely. Will there be months where you want to just be a "pew warmer" and go through the motions? Most individuals experience something like that during their lives. But remember, God wants faithful servants who persevere unto death. "And you will be hated by all for My name's sake. But he who endures to the end will be saved" (Matthew 10:22). Consider what Jesus wrote to the faithful church in Philadelphia who did not deny His name: "Because you have kept My command to persevere, I also will keep you from the hour of trial which shall come upon the whole world" (Revelation 3:10).

Who do you know that matches the definition of true success?

That's why the person you pick to marry is so critically important. This is the person who will be running this marathon race with you. On your good days you may have to lift them up. On your bad days he or she can lift you up. But you keep running - with purpose, determination, and passion. Paul, in writing to young Timothy, declared, "I have fought the good fight, I have finished the race, I have kept the faith. Finally, there is laid up for me the crown of righteousness, which the Lord, the righteous Judge, will give to me on that Day, and not to me only but also to all who have loved His appearing" (2 Timothy 4:7-8).

As you consider your Christian walk, never take your eyes off the finish line. Never forget that you must cross that line before resting. Always remember the words of Revelation 2:10, "... Be faithful until death, and I will give you the crown of life."If I had it my way, the day you step out into eternity you would still be running—only to collapse in the arms of Abraham. Push on!

Verses for Further Study

| Luke 8:14 | Matthew 10:22 | 2 Timothy 4:7-8 |
| John 6:66 | Revelation 3:10 | Revelation 2:10 |

Finishing the Course • Christian Character

Holiness

One of the biggest questions plaguing congregations all across the globe is, "How can we increase our numbers?" At a time in which many church families are either declining or simply swapping members with other congregations, many have turned to all kinds of programs and gimmicks to attract people. In addition, many church leaders have shifted money away from mission work and external outreach, and instead, are focusing much of the churches resources inwardly. But how many congregations are focusing on the spiritual health of their own members?

The Bible records over and over that we are to be holy or sanctified. Sadly, many congregations have lost their passion for holiness. Some of these congregations have focused **all** of their attention on getting worship "right" rather than getting those who worship right. (Just to clarify, I do insist worship should be done right—but is it possible in some cases that have we gotten the letter of the law right to the neglect of the actions and attitudes of the worshippers?) Other congregations have turned toward entertainment in an effort to please the masses.

Here's what I intend to teach my children regarding holiness.

Being a Christian is more than just checking off a box on Sunday and Wednesday. It is my prayer that while you will seek to worship and praise God on Sunday, that you will also devote your life to Him, seek to serve Him, and to be holy. Holiness and sanctification are a part of what should define you as a Christian. Pursue peace with all people, and holiness, without which no one will see the Lord (Hebrews 12:14).

If everyone who wanted to go to Heaven ended up there, it would soon be full of adulterers, murders, slanderers, and the like. Imagine what Heaven would soon be like! Only those who are holy will be there, as God cannot have anything to do with sin and still be God. But here is the catch — man is unable to be holy on his own.

Holiness • Christian Character

It is only through the spotless Lamb of Christ that God can see us and **treat us** as holy. Look at what the prophet Isaiah wrote: "A highway shall be there, and a road, and it shall be called the Highway of Holiness. The unclean shall not pass over it" (Isaiah 35:9). In verse nine the prophet continued, "But the redeemed shall walk there." Will there be murderers, adulterers, and slanderers in Heaven? Yes, but they will be individuals who were washed with the blood of Jesus and gave up their sinful ways to pursue holiness.

To be holy means we are "in Christ." Look at how Paul addressed those in Corinth: "To the church of God which is at Corinth, to those who are *sanctified in Christ Jesus,* called to be saints" (1 Corinthians 1:2, emp. added). To the church at Rome Paul wrote, "being justified freely by His grace through the redemption that is **in Christ Jesus**" (Romans 3:24, emp. added). Do a word study and notice how many times the Scriptures mention being "in Christ."

God is the source of holiness. The Greek root word for holy is *hagios,* and means "likeness of nature with the Lord." The way I want you to remember holiness is this: holiness moves you away from sin and moves you toward God. If you are going to be holy, you must conform your heart and life to God. You must also conform to the examples set forth by Jesus Christ. And you must be willing to conform to the laws and commands of God. "Therefore gird up the loins of your mind, be sober, and rest your hope fully upon the grace that is to be brought to you at the revelation of Jesus Christ; as obedient children, not conforming yourselves to the former lusts, as in your ignorance; but as He who called you is holy, you also be holy in all your conduct, because it is written, 'Be holy, for I am holy'" (1 Peter 1:13-16).

This same sentiment was given to God's chosen people in the Old Testament:

> For I am the Lord your God. You shall therefore consecrate yourselves, and you shall be holy; for I am holy. Neither shall you defile yourselves with any creeping thing that creeps on the earth. For I am the Lord who brings you up out of the land of Egypt, to be your God. You shall therefore be holy, for I am holy (Leviticus 11:44-45).

Realize that today you are God's chosen people. "But you are a chosen generation, a *royal priesthood,* a holy nation, His own special people, that you may proclaim the praises of Him who called you out of darkness into His marvelous light" (1 Peter 2:9).

Holiness • Christian Character

I'm not sure why Christians don't pursue holiness like they did in the past. Maybe it is because we have lost confidence in the authority of Scripture. I suspect some of it has to do with the reality that most people (even Christians) don't think they are that bad, and thus we are not thankful for the gift Christ provides. Or maybe it is because the bar seems too high. Or maybe we have been deluded by the Father of Lies. Personally, I believe some of it is that Christians today have become more comfortable with conforming to the world and thus we have an absence of strong role models to follow. I'm afraid this lack of holiness is part of why the church has been declining. If we want our congregations to grow, then we must make sure the members are spiritually healthy.

As you continue to grow up, please do not forget holiness—remember what Christ did for you on the cross. Don't return back to sin, but rather strive to be like Christ. Paul wrote, "Therefore, having these promises, beloved, let us cleanse ourselves from all filthiness of the flesh and spirit, perfecting holiness in the fear of God" (2 Corinthians 7:1). Strive to be different. Do not conform to the world. I'll leave you with one of our favorite passages: "And do not be **conformed to this world**, but be **transformed** by the renewing of your mind, that you may prove what is that good and acceptable and perfect will of God." Remember you can't do it without Christ — never forget that He must be your example. This is a lesson that I still work on every day.

Family Discussion

HOW IMPORTANT IS OUR ATTITUDE WHEN IT COMES TO OBEDIENCE?

Verses for Further Study

Hebrews 12:14	Romans 3:24	1 Peter 2:9
Isaiah 35:9	1 Peter 1:13-16	2 Corinthians 7:1
1 Corinthians 1:2	Leviticus 11:44-45	

Gentleness

Proverbs 15:1 states, "A soft answer turns away wrath, but a harsh word stirs up anger." While we know this intellectually, sometimes, in our humanness, we find being gentle much harder than lashing out. Gentleness is described as one of the fruits of the Spirit (Galatians 5:22-23), but the honest truth is, sometimes, men (and women) find it hard to exhibit this important trait.

Oftentimes, gentleness is perceived as weakness. I am now convinced that gentleness requires even more strength than lashing out. Jesus is a great example of someone who possessed enormous power but was still able to give a soft touch. Paul observed, "Now I, Paul, myself am pleading with you, by the meekness and gentleness of Christ—who in presence am lowly among you, but being absent am bold toward you" (2 Corinthians 10:1). It's a trait our Master Teacher held, but one we don't discuss often from the pulpit.

Here is what I intend to teach my children about gentleness.

If you were to ask some of my close friends, gentleness is not a word that immediately comes to mind in describing me. In fact, your mom has, on more than one occasion, called me a "bull in a china shop." I tend to be much more like Peter than Paul when it comes to my actions. That was clearly seen when the Lord blessed me with two boys. For many years I would roll around in the floor with you. I can still hear your mom telling me that I was being "too rough" with her little baby boys. In fact, I suspect we both carry physical scars of epic battles that got a little out of control.

But God, in His infinite wisdom, knew exactly what I needed to help learn gentleness. He blessed our family with a little girl. I grew up in a family with two older brothers - so having a little girl around was totally foreign. Suddenly I was walking around on eggshells. My whole world was turned upside down. All the swords and guns were replaced with dolls, hair barrettes, and horses. And little by little I began to learn more about gentleness.

Gentleness • Christian Character

57

Money and prestige don't buy gentleness. Gentleness is something we must learn and work on in order to be more like Christ. Gentleness must come from the heart. After pointing out that the love of money is a root of all kinds of evil, Paul told Timothy, "But you, O man of God, flee these things and pursue righteousness, godliness, faith, love, patience, gentleness" (1 Timothy 6:10-11). In his letter to the church at Philippi, Paul admonished, "Let your gentleness be known to all men. The Lord is at hand" (Philippians 4:5).

What I had not learned before your sister came along was that it is easy (and worldly) to be brash or even rough. Gentleness, however, takes strength and reflects Christ back to the world. For you see, I didn't suddenly lose all my strength when Claire was born - rather I learned how to harness that strength into a soft and gentle touch.

We are commanded that if someone is overtaken in any trespass we are to restore him "in a spirit of gentleness" (Galatians 6:1). Paul wrote: "I, therefore, the prisoner of the Lord, beseech you to walk worthy of the calling with which you were called, with all lowliness and gentleness, with longsuffering, bearing with one another in love, endeavoring to keep the unity of the Spirit in the bond of peace (Ephesians 4:1-3)."

Two times in the Old Testament the Bible records, "You have also given me the shield of Your salvation; Your right hand has held me up, Your gentleness has made me great" (Psalm 18:35; 2 Samuel 22:36).

You might be asking at this point: why? Why do I need to pursue gentleness? Ultimately, the answer lies in Christ—our redeemer and example. Paul summed it up well when he wrote, "For the kingdom of God is not in word but in power. What do you want? Shall I come to you with a rod, or in love and a spirit of gentleness?" (1 Corinthians 4:20-21). Thankfully we serve a God who has all power in His hand— but thanks to Christ, His "touch" is not one of force, but rather, one of gentleness. This is one of those traits that may take you a little while. However, the sooner you learn this truth - the better your life will be.

Verses for Further Study

Proverbs 15:1	Philippians 4:5	2 Samuel 22:36
Galatians 5:22-23	Galatians 6:1	1 Corinthians
2 Corinthians 10:1	Ephesians 4:1-3	4:20-21
1 Timothy 6:10-11	Psalm 18:35	

Gentleness • Christian Character

58

Generosity

The world is watching. They might not admit it, but they are watching. Non-Christians like to see if Christians really "walk the walk." Yes, they have heard about our Jesus, but they want to know if you will really help them when they need it. Will you really mow their grass when they are out of town? Will you really come by the hospital when their child is sick? Will you really give of your time and money to help those who are less fortunate?

For many years, the church did not do so well at serving others. Sure, we talked about it from the pulpit, but it didn't go much further than that. Oftentimes, we justified our lack of service or generosity by saying we had given when the collection was taken up on Sunday. As a result, many Christians grew comfortable not doing much outside the building. It was during this time that many skeptics and agnostics hurled words like "hypocrites" or "charlatans" at the Christian community.

Enter the millennial generation. This younger generation realized that their parents did not always "do" what they were saying. They found this troubling and set out to change things. Many millennials are very service-oriented, generous, and they are not as interested in climbing the corporate ladder like previous generations. The church badly needs to harness their energy and attitude when it comes to generosity and service!

Here's what I intend to teach my children about generosity.

When I was young, my dad had a bumper sticker on one of our cars that said, "Practice random acts of kindness." Those words stuck—in a huge way. What I learned very quickly is that those acts of generosity usually make the giver feel better than the recipient does by receiving the gift. I had the privilege of seeing this on a mission trip to a third-world country. We brought some of your own stuffed animals to give

Generosity • Christian Character

to the children where we were working. Initially, you were troubled about the thought of giving up those stuffed animals. But when you witnessed first-hand how much joy they brought to children who would otherwise never have stuffed animals, you made the comment that we should have brought more. It was in that moment that I knew you had experienced the joy of being a giver. The writer of Proverbs observed, "One gives freely, yet grows all the richer; another withholds what he should give, and only suffers want" (Proverbs 11:24).

It is my hope that you will grow up to be givers. Paul observed, "I have shown you in every way, by laboring like this, that you must support the weak. And remember the words of the Lord Jesus, that He said, 'It is more blessed to give than to receive'" (Acts 20:35). The first century church was built on the concept of Christians selling what they had to give to those who were in need (Acts 2:45).

Understand this is not what the world is going to tell you. The world is going to tell you that everything is all about you—and that you should have more, better, newer, etc. And maybe that's why giving is so rewarding today—it is so unexpected from individuals in our culture. Learn to listen and look for opportunities to give.

Why am I asking you to be generous? Because it demonstrates to others the love of God. We read in 1 John 3:17, "But whoever has this world's goods, and sees his brother in need, and shuts up his heart from him, how does the love of God abide in him?" Giving to others with a generous spirit is a reminder that your treasures are in Heaven, not here on earth. It also helps remind us that all of this "stuff" around us, is just that—stuff. You are never too young to learn this important trait. Practice giving and make sure generosity is a part of your lifestyle.

Individual Question

HOW CAN YOU PERSONALLY BECOME MORE GENEROUS?

Verses for Further Study			
Prov 11:24	Acts 20:35	Acts 2:45	1 John 3:17

Self-Control

Judas did not possess it. Neither did David. In fact, had Adam and Eve possessed more of it, we might not be in the mess we find ourselves today. What is "it"? Self-control. Simply put, we do not like telling ourselves "no."

Here's what I intend to teach my children about self-control.

When you get older you will discover that you have the ability to sit down and binge on 12 hours of Netflix movies or eat an entire container of Oreos (or, in my case, ice cream!). However, while that option exists to adults, it does not mean those are healthy or productive choices. Instead, you must train yourself to have discipline and only eat 2-3 Oreos. This discipline is known as "self-control" and it is one of the fruits of the Spirit (Galatians 5:22-23). Proverbs 25:28 says, "Whoever has no rule over his own spirit is like a city broken down, without walls."

The Christian life is a disciplined life. You are not your own. You were bought with a price (1 Corinthians 6:19-20). One of the toughest things you will learn after you leave the home is how to discipline yourself with all your newfound freedoms. Every day you will discover you must choose—choose between the narrow path and the broad way. Be prepared to train yourself and limit yourself.

In the 1980s, there was a flurry of scientific studies published about the addicitive properties of drugs such as cocaine. One of the studies used rats that were tethered

One of the toughest things you will learn after you leave the home is how to discipline yourself with all your newfound freedoms.

61

in their cages and rigged to self-administer cocaine by pressing a lever. The researchers discovered that rats that were isolated would continue to self-administer cocaine until they died (*Bozarth and Wise 1985*). Rats that were not isolated and had things to play with, did not use cocaine to the same degree. Think about that—rats that had better things to think about and had companions, were not as likely to overdose on cocaine.

In a Stanford research study years earlier, Walter Mischel studied children and their reaction to an instant small reward or two rewards later if they waited a short period of time (15 minutes). This study is often referred to as the "Marshmallow Test" because the rewards offered to children were often marshmallows. One of the most unique aspects of this research was that years later Mischel did a follow up study and discovered that the children who demonstrated delayed gratification also did considerably better on the SAT, performed better in school, and had overall better life outcomes.

Mischel's "Marshmallow Test" demonstrated that self-control can be learned. Children would often look at the reward differently. In a *New York Times* piece, Mischel observed,

> "The children who succeed turn their backs on the cookie, push it away, pretend it's something nonedible like a piece of wood, or invent a song. Instead of staring down the cookie, they transform it into something with less of a throbbing pull on them ... If you change how you think about it, its' impact on what you feel and do changes"[1].

In other words, it is how you view something. You must be willing to battle. Consider this—God gave the Israelites the Promised Land, but they still had to battle for it. Self-control is similar in that you will often have an internal battle. You must therefore train yourself to have self-control.

Paul describes running the race striving for the crown, "And everyone who competes for the prize is temperate in all things. Now they do it to obtain a perishable crown, but we for an imperishable crown. Therefore I run thus: not with uncertainty. Thus I fight: not as one who beats the air. But I discipline my body and bring it into subjection, lest, when I have preached to others, I myself should become disqualified." 1 Corinthians 9:25-27).

Peter wrote, "But also for this very reason, giving all diligence, add to your faith virtue, to virtue knowledge, to knowledge self-control, to self-control perseverance, to perseverance godliness, to godliness brotherly kindness, and to brotherly kindness love. For if these things are yours and abound, you will be neither barren nor unfruitful in the knowledge of our Lord Jesus Christ." (2 Peter 1:5-8).

It is my prayer that as you mature and grow in Him you will also grow in self-control. Keep working and keep at it. I guarantee it will be worth it in the end!

Questions

WHAT CAN YOU DO TO ENCOURAGE GREATER SELF-CONTROL?

HOW CAN YOU ENCOURAGE THOSE AROUND YOU TO EXERSIZE GREATER CONTROL?

WHAT ARE SOME IMMEDIATE BENEFITS OF GOOD SELF-CONTROL?

Verses for Further Study

Galatians 5:22-23	1 Corinthians 9:25-27
Proverbs 25:28	2 Peter 1:5-8
1 Corinthians 6:19-20	

[1] https://www.nytimes. com/2014/09/14/opinion/sunday/learning-self-control. html?mcubz=0

63

Singing

There is a great deal that evolutionists proclaim nature can explain. Textbooks drone on about how "under the right conditions" this could have done that. Or they imply relationships that in reality are only real on paper. Darwinians declare that natural selection — survival of the fittest — along with time and mutations can explain everything without a supernatural creator. While there are many problems with their theory, consider one area that is rarely touched by evolutionists: music. How can "survival of the fittest" explain the origin of music and singing?

Music and songs have the ability to touch the core of mankind. They can evoke emotions that words alone cannot. They can literally change our moods. Songs have the ability to bring tears to our eyes and smiles to our faces. It is no wonder then that singing is a very vital part of the way we worship to God. But are we really singing with the right heart and spirit? A casual glance around an auditorium on a Sunday morning reveals that not everyone is singing. Often times, older men will sit with arms folded glaring straight ahead. Or you might see groups of teens standing, either not moving their lips, or barely mouthing the words.

Here's what I intend to teach my children on the topic of singing.

There are some areas that God has blessed me with specific talents. Singing, as you well know, is not one of those areas. (Stop smiling!) You have, on many occasions, been blessed with my "melodious" voice crooning out of the shower—while your mom buries her head in the pillow and dogs in the neighborhood begin howling. Yeah, it's that bad.

However, I never want you to forget that even though that is not one of my talents, I still am thankful to be able to sing praises to God. Paul wrote, "What is the conclusion then? I will pray with the spirit, and I will also pray with the understanding. I will sing with the spirit, and

Singing • Church Life

I will also sing with the understanding"(1 Corinthians 14:15). Part of your task of worshipping in spirit and truth (John 4:24) is to open your mouth and sing.

Some of my sweetest memories are long car trips with everyone singing. Those are special times that I hope you never forget—and I hope you pass them on to your children. While I hope you received your mom's singing ability, whether or not you are "good" is not important to the Creator who framed you and gave you your voice. The Scriptures teach that we all play a vital part and that together we are the body: "If the whole body were an eye, where would the sense of hearing be? If the whole body were an ear, where would the sense of smell be? But in fact God has placed the parts in the body, every one of them, just as He wanted them to be. If they were all one part, where would the body be? As it is, there are many parts, but one body." (1 Corinthians 12:15-20).

God does not look at things the same way humans do (1 Samuel 16:7). This isn't about entertainment or some kind of singing competition. This is about being pleasing to the Lord. We are commanded to sing praises to God. This is one of the ways we get to demonstrate to Him our love. Paul admonished: "Let the word of Christ dwell in you richly in all wisdom, teaching and admonishing one another in psalms and hymns and spiritual songs, singing with grace in your hearts to the Lord" (Colossians 3:16). Remember the words of the writer of Hebrews who observed:"Therefore by Him let us continually offer the sacrifice of praise to God, that is, the fruit of our lips, giving thanks to His name" (Hebrews 13:15). Don't grumble and say, "I don't know the words of this song." Remember all songs were new at some point.

Consider for a moment how you would feel if you were the only one singing in an auditorium full of people. The sight of all of the people with tightly closed lips would probably be very disheartening. Your voice, when blended with the voices of other Christians, is a beautiful sound to the Lord, and it also serves as an encouragement to those around you. Paul affirmed, "Speaking to one another in psalms and hymns and spiritual songs, singing and making melody in your heart to the Lord" (Ephesians 5:19). So open your mouth, open your heart, and make a joyful noise to the Lord.

Verses for Further Study

1 Corinthians 12:15-20; 14:15	Colossians 3:16
John 4:24	Hebrews 13:15
1 Samuel 16:7	Ephesians 5:19

Singing • Church Life

The 10 Commandments

They are not as common as they used to be. Twenty-five years ago you could find the Ten Commandments posted in various places of business or even classrooms. Today, the very sight of the Ten Commandments draws harsh words and lawsuits. More and more businesses and public places are removing the commands for fear of vitriol from the ACLU. This militant "anti-God" pursuit has caused an unexpected backlash. Many in the denominational world have put up yard signs containing the Ten Commandments. Many congregations have encouraged their members to display them proudly at homes or in private businesses in an effort to stem the immoral tide of our nation.

Children reared in Christian homes are not blind to the fight going on around them. They hear news accounts each month over the battle. They are acutely aware that the commandments are no longer allowed in school classrooms. They sit in Bible classes that discuss each individual command. But sadly, many children never understand what the Law of Moses means to a New Testament Christian.

Here's what I intend on teaching my children about the Ten Commandments and the Old Law.

The Ten Commandments are a part of God's inspired Word, and they are definitely something we can learn from (Romans 15:4). It doesn't bother me to see them posted, other than it makes me realize that someone only knows part of the beautiful story God has painted for us today! I am extremely thankful that Jesus nailed that Old Law to the cross (Colossians 2:13-14). That Old Law served a purpose in God's plan. It was designed to help purify a nation and lead them toward Christ. In addition, it set God as the standard for right and wrong and reminded individuals of their transgressions (Galatians 3:19-25). But that Old Law had a problem, as it could not take away sins (Hebrews 10:1-4).

While some associate the Law of Moses with just ten "Thou shall not ..." commandments (found in Exodus 20), there were actually many more instructions mentioned. Those commands were given to Moses on stone tablets written by the finger of God (Exodus 31:18). The Ten Commandments we read in Exodus 20, were the principles that God would then expound on. We can find additional laws throughout the latter part of Exodus and in the books of Leviticus and Numbers. God was trying to demonstrate what was unclean and sinful to these people—but it could not justify the people of that day (Galatians 3:10-13). As such, the Old Law was a temporary law that was given to the Israelites. Think of it like this: A new section of multi-lane interstate is being built. But while it is under construction there is a bumpy and temporary pathway around to the other side. Only one group of people got to use that bumpy, "under construction" path. That's what the Old Law was like. When Jesus died, He tore down the "under construction" sign permanently, got rid of that old bumpy path, and He opened up a beautiful stretch of interstate available to everyone.

That's why I'm thankful that we live under a new covenant—it is open to Jew and Gentile! The Bible says Jesus has become a surety of a **better** covenant (Hebrews 7:22). For it is the blood of Christ that is able to wash away sins. Take a close look at the following Scriptures: 1 Peter 1:18-19; 1 John 1:7; Revelation 1:5. In His final act on earth, Jesus tore off the yoke of bondage which was from the Old Law that had been on the Jewish people (Galatians 5:1).

You might ask: Are we still under the Ten Commandments today? Let me answer with another question: Would you still want to use that old bumpy, "under construction" pathway when you have access to a beautiful new paved interstate? Today we are free from the Old Law (Romans 7:1-6). Some might say we still follow nine of the original Ten Commands. How can we follow something if Jesus nailed it to the cross and we are free from it? What these individuals mean is that the New Law records for us nine of the same principles/commands.

As you study the Old Testament, I pray that you will gain a greater understanding of what was required under the Law of Moses. For if you understand the Old Law, you will have a much better appreciation and understanding of what Jesus did for you. You will also have a bigger appreciation for a God who has had a redemptive plan for you since the creation of the world!

Verses for Further Study

Romans 7:1-6, 15:4	Hebrews 7:22; 10:1-4	1 John 1:7
Colossians 2:13-14	Exodus 20; 31:18	Revelation 1:5
Gal. 3:10-13; 5:1; 19-25	1 Peter 1:18-19	

The 10 Commandments and the Old Law • Church Life

Angels

At a very young age children learn about the birth of Jesus. They hear about how the angel Gabriel came to Mary to announce that she would bring forth a Son and His name would be Jesus (Luke 1:26-31). They are told about the angel of the Lord appearing to the shepherds announcing: "For there is born to you this day in the city of David a Savior, who is Christ the Lord. 12 And this will be the sign to you: You will find a Babe wrapped in swaddling cloths, lying in a manger" (Luke 2:11-12).

Our children's introduction to angels often occurs early in their Biblical training. They learn of the cheribum that was placed "at the east of the garden of Eden" to guard the way to the tree of life after Adam and Eve were put out of the garden (Genesis 3:24). They listen to sermons about Isaiah reporting seeing seraphim around the throne of the Lord (Isaiah 6:1-2) and they hear about other angels such as Michael (Daniel 10:13).

Add to this, they are often confronted with angel figurines in stores or in television shows. By the age of ten, most children are familiar with the term angel, but they have lots of questions about them.

Unfortunately, in the church we often steer clear from things that we either don't fully understand or things that are not physical in nature. The scientific community has done a great job of convincing us that if we can't measure things with our five senses then they are not real. And thus, most young people transition from childhood into adulthood without ever having their questions answered.

Here's what I intend to teach my children about angels.

Angels are real, and it excites me to be able to tell you that one day you will understand them completely. The Greek word *angelos* is translated angels or messengers. Having said that, I want to tell each one of you there are many things your mom and dad don't know—and

68

that is okay. The Bible even records that some "secret things belong to the Lord our God," (Deuteronomy 29:29). However, on the topic of angels there are many things we do know, and I encourage you to study these special beings.

For instance, we know they are not eternal beings—but rather they are created. Nehemiah 9:6 records "You alone are the Lord; You have made heaven, the heaven of heavens, with all their hosts, the earth and everything on it, the seas and all that is in them. And You preserved them all, the host of heaven worships You." Psalm 148 also reminds us of this point (see verse 2 and verse 5; see also Colossians 1:16-17). Additionally, we are told, "For in six days the Lord made the heavens and the earth, the sea, and all that is in them, and rested the seventh day" (Exodus 20:11).

If angels are not eternal, then they were a part of God's creation. In Job 38, we learn that the "sons of God" (translated angels) were present when God laid the foundations of the earth (v. 7). Thus, if they were here when God laid the foundations of the earth, and they are created beings, then one could conclude that they were created by God on day one before the foundation of the earth was laid.

Often referred to as ministering spirits (e.g., Hebrews 1:14) they do not have bodies like humans and are not given in marriage like humans (Matthew 22:30). However, we believe they can take the appearance of men (e.g., Hebrews 13:2).

While the Bible does not indicate how many there are, it does on several occasions mention that the total number is great (see Matthew 26:53; Hebrews 12:22) Additionally, the Bible reveals some details about what they are able to do.

In the Old Testament we read that the "angel of the Lord" killed 185,000 Assyrians (2 Kings 19:35). We also learn in Matthew 28:2 that it was an angel of the Lord who "descended from heaven, and came and rolled back the stone" from Jesus' tomb.

The Bible records that it was an angel of the Lord who "opened the prison doors and brought them out" (Acts 5:19). It was an angel who was able to get Peter out of prison (Acts 12:7) and then later struck Herod (Acts 12:23). And finally we know that when Jesus is revealed from heaven he will be joined by His "mighty angels" (2 Thessalonians 1:7).

For now I will close with two interesting things to consider. First,

Angels • Church Life

Jesus observed, "Take heed that you do not despise one of these little ones, for I say to you that in heaven their angels always see the face of My Father who is in heaven" (Matthew 18:10).

Second, the writer of Hebrews noted, "Do not forget to entertain strangers, for by so doing some have unwittingly entertained angels" (Hebrews 13:2). Interesting to think about, isn't it? Angels are fascinating beings that play a very special role in the universe God created.

Verses for Further Study

Luke 1:26-31; 2:11-12	Job 38
Genesis 3:24	Hebrews 1:14; 12:22; 13:2
Daniel 10:13	2 Kings 19:35
Isaiah 6:1-2	Matthew 18:10; 22:30;
Deut 29:29	26:53; 28:2
Nehemiah 9:6	Acts 5:19; 12:7, 23
Psalm 148	2 Thessalonians 1:7
Colossians 1:16-17	
Exodus 20:11	

Angels • Church Life

Angels Part 2

I always get nervous when I walk into a home that is filled with angel figurines. Maybe it is the high probability that I will break one or maybe it is the appearance that these figures are almost worshipped. Angels are everywhere—in media, advertising, in books, in artwork, and in the Bible. This chapter we will continue our discussion of angels.

Here's more of what I intend to teach my children about angels.

One of the passages of Scripture that has always intrigued me is when Jesus was in the Garden of Gethsemane praying, and the Lord sent an angel to strengthen Him (Luke 22:43). It appears from Scripture that angels are stronger physically than humans. In 2 Peter 2:11 we read, "Whereas angels, who are greater in power and might, do not bring a reviling accusation against them before the Lord."

Remember, it was an angel of the Lord who rolled away the stone of Jesus' tomb (Matthew 28:2). The inspired psalmist observed, "Bless the Lord, you His angels, who excel in strength, who do His word, heeding the voice of His word" (Psalm 103:20).

It is also apparent from Scripture that angels have intelligence, wisdom, and the ability to understand. For instance, when Jesus was talking about His coming again, He noted: "But of that day and hour no one knows, not even the angels of heaven, but My Father only" (Matthew 24:36; see also 2 Samuel 14:20).

Consider what Gabriel told Daniel regarding the seventy weeks prophecy: "And he informed me, and talked with me, and said, 'O Daniel, I have now come forth to give you skill to understand. At the beginning of your supplications the command went out, and I have come to tell you, for you are greatly beloved; therefore consider the matter, and understand the vision'" (Daniel 9:22-23).

While they may be strong, they apparently are not above temptation. While I can't give you the specific cause, their strength and wisdom may have played a role is causing a group of angels to be cast down— my suspicion is that they wanted to be like God. We can be assured that upon the completion of God's creation that everything was very good (Genesis 1:31).

Yet, at some point in time between Genesis 1:31 and Genesis 3 we recognize that Satan became evil and tempted Adam and Eve. The Bible speaks of the devil and his angels (Matthew 25:41). To get a better understanding of this fall we can turn to 2 Peter 2:4 where we learn, "For if God did not spare the angels who sinned, but cast them down to hell and delivered them into chains of darkness, to be reserved for judgment."

We also know, "And the angels who did not keep their proper domain, but left their own abode, He has reserved in everlasting chains under darkness for the judgment of the great day" (Jude 6; see also Ephesians 6:12). The Bible is replete with the reality that demons plagued the earth.

This was not God's original plan for angels—angels have several roles in God's greater plan. To comprehend better their "work," consider Isaiah 6:1-3, where they are worshipping and praising God. We also find in Daniel 6 that an angel was sent to shut the mouths of the lions and protect Daniel (6:23). According to Scripture, in the account of the rich man and Lazarus, the beggar was carried by angels to Abraham's bosom upon his death (Luke 16:22), so they probably play a ministering role with our spirits upon our death.

Recall that it was an angel who ministered to Hagar in Genesis 21:17-18, after Abraham sent Hagar and Ishmael into the wilderness. It was also an angel who cared for Elijah under the broom tree (1 Kings 19:5-7). They also serve as messengers/guides (e.g., Joseph in the birth of Jesus, Matthew 1:20-25; angels appearing to shepherds in the field, Luke 2:9-15).

One role that we commonly don't think about is they help reveal God's law. In Acts 7:52-53 we read, "Which of the prophets did your fathers not persecute? And they killed those who foretold the coming of the Just One, of whom you now have become the betrayers and murderers, who have received the law by the direction of angels and have not kept it."

Consider also that it was an angel that appeared to Cornelius to tell him to send for Peter to discover what he—as a Gentile—needed to do in order to obey God and be saved (Acts 10:3-6).

I recognize you might still have questions regarding these special creations. There will be a day in the future when the "curtain will be pulled back" and you will learn a great deal more. Keep striving for Heaven so that you will have that special opportunity.

Verses for Further Study

Luke 2:9-15; 16:22; 22:43	Genesis 1:31; 3
2 Peter 2:11	Jude 6
Psalm 103:20	Ephesians 6:12
Matthew 1:20-25; 24:36	Isaiah 6:1-3
Matthew 25:41; 28:2	Genesis 21:17-18
2 Samuel 14:20	1 Kings 19:5-7
Daniel 6; 9:22-23	Acts 7:52-53; 10:3-6

Angels Part 2 • Church Life

The Scariest Verse in the Bible

Humanism can be defined as a system of thought that rejects religious beliefs and centers on humans, their values, capacities, and worth. It is a belief system that places humans at the top. In a "politically correct" era when people demand a "separation of church and state," humanism has become the backbone for most modern-day textbooks. History is not taught in terms of God being the founder of the world, but rather, our children learning about the "Big Bang" and Neanderthal man. The complexity and purposeful design of nature is ignored—as it would demand a designer. Instead our children are indoctrinated by evolutionary theory and naturalism.

But these theories in-and-of-themselves are not the whole problem. For you see, a steady diet of humanism causes individuals to think more highly of themselves—after all, humanism teaches we are at the top. This has resulted in a generation of "self" oriented young people who believe they and their opinions are extremely important (e.g., sharing their every move on Facebook or Twitter). It has also resulted in an overabundance of narcissists.

This humanistic attitude has even crept into the church. We throw labels around like "righteous" and "godly" on individuals without really considering what we are saying. We use the label "sinners" with such ease that we don't really even feel any discomfort. After all, we're not that bad, right?

Here's what I intend to teach my children about the scariest verse in the Bible.

The Bible is filled with all kinds of fighting action and gruesome deaths. But I want to take a moment to share with you what I hope you will remember as the scariest verse in the Bible. In Mark 10:18 we read, "So Jesus said to him, "Why do you call Me good? No one is good but One, that is, God." Not exactly what you were expecting was it? But look at that passage again. God is good! And still you say, "Yeah, what's the problem?" The problem is you are not good.

In Isaiah 64:6 we read, "But we are all like an unclean thing, and all our righteousnesses are like filthy rags; we all fade as a leaf, and our iniquities, like the wind, have taken us away." Paul put it this way in his letter to the church at Rome: "As it is written: 'There is none righteous, no, not one.'" (Romans 3:10). In 1 John the Bible says, "If we say that we have no sin, we deceive ourselves, and the truth is not in us" (1 John 1:8).

Let me point it out again: God is good. But we are not. So the question you should be asking yourself is: What does a good God do with us? This is where the term "good news" comes into play. This is the essence of the Gospel message. Sadly, because of our affection for humanism and "self," the good news isn't viewed as all that good anymore. After all, we really aren't that bad ... right?

In Exodus 34:6-7, God gives us a picture of Himself. (Anytime you want to know more about God it is always a good thing to go to Scripture rather than man!) The Bible says, "And the Lord passed before him and proclaimed, 'The Lord, the Lord God, merciful and gracious, longsuffering, and abounding in goodness and truth, keeping mercy for thousands, forgiving iniquity and transgression and sin.'" Those words are tremendous and comforting! We learn God is merciful and gracious. But the passage does not stop there. It continues by saying: "by no means clearing the guilty, visiting the iniquity of the fathers upon the children and the children's children to the third and the fourth generation." (Exodus 34:6-7). How can that be? How can He be merciful and forgiving, but then not clear the guilty?

I want you to think about this dilemma for just a moment. We expect judges to be fair and to deliver penalties according to the crime. And yet, we don't want God to hold us responsible for all of the sin we have committed. How can a good God overlook our sin? Paul explains this in Romans 3.

"For all have sinned and fall short of the glory of God, being justified freely by His grace through the redemption that is in Christ Jesus, whom God set forth as a propitiation by His blood, through faith, to demonstrate His righteousness, because in His forbearance God had passed over the sins that were previously committed" (Romans 3:23-25).

Paul then goes on to use a very special phrase to describe God, continuing this passage by saying, "to demonstrate at the present time

The Scariest Verse in the Bible •Church Life

75

His righteousness, that He might be just and the justifier of the one who has faith in Jesus." (v. 26). Look at that phrase just a moment: just and justifier.

If God were only just, then every human would be punished in eternity for all the sins they have committed — as He is holy and cannot have anything to do with sin. But the text says He was also the justifier. That was Jesus Christ — and that is GREAT news!

The next time you think highly of yourself take a moment to ask yourself who are you comparing yourself to? Are you comparing yourself with an ungodly world, or with a holy God? Never, ever forget that without the blood of Jesus Christ — the spotless sacrifice — you are nothing. Only God is good ...

Questions

CAN YOU THINK OF A TIME YOU GOT INTO TROUBLE OR AN UNCOMFORTABLE SITUATION BECAUSE YOU THOUGHT TOO HIGHLY OF YOURSELF?

HOW CAN YOU KEEP IN MIND THAT ONLY GOD IS GOOD?

Verses for Further Study

| Mark 10:18 | Romans 3:10, 23-26 | Exodus 34:6-7 |
| Isaiah 64:6 | 1 John 1:8 | |

Works Righteousness

Humans have a propensity towards "works righteousness." We may not want to believe it, but deep down, most of us think we are playing a major role in our salvation. I think many Christians acknowledge the role Jesus Christ plays in our salvation, but the reality is, we scour the Scripture to find things "to do" and then work really hard believing we play an important role.

Often, our works righteousness attitude is grown out of fear or pride. For those who live their lives in fear, every time something bad happens they believe it is because of something they did (or didn't do well enough). They honestly believe their own actions brought about the "bad" thing. Friends, that would mean that for every day that they experienced something "good" they would honestly believe they earned/deserved it. That is not how God works and it is not God's plan for man's salvation.

Likewise, there are many who have the attitude, "Thank you, Jesus, for dying on the cross. Now, look at all this stuff I've done to add to your sacrifice." A lot of this arrogance is fed by the church and is supported by the humanistic/narcissistic egotism that is prevalent today.

Here's what I intend to teach my children regarding works righteousness.

At your very best, you will be nothing but a filthy rag compared to God. I don't say that to hurt your feelings. I tell you that so that you can always keep the proper perspective of who God is and who you are. (You know we have not been parents who pamper and build false self-esteem.) Allow me to back up what I said with Scripture: "But we are all like an unclean thing, and all our righteousnesses are like filthy rags; We all fade as a leaf, and our iniquities, like the wind, have taken

77

us away" (Isaiah 64:6). God is telling you that at your very best you are nothing but a nasty pile of rags. Paul wrote, "As it is written, There is none righteous, no, not one" (Romans 3:10). A few verses later he added, "for all have sinned and fall short of the glory of God" (Romans 3:23). In other words, you ain't all that.

There are many people who will be uncomfortable with what we are teaching you, because they honestly believe they can — by their own hands — add to what Jesus did on the cross. But the reality is, salvation is only through Jesus Christ (see Acts 4:12; John 14:6). You are unable to add to His sacrifice and grace. Many people comprehend this intellectually, but their gut still tells them they must check off so many boxes in order to be a godly Christian and go to Heaven. Listen to what Paul wrote to Titus,

> "Not by works of righteousness which we have done, but according to His mercy He saved us, through the washing of regeneration and renewing of the Holy Spirit, whom He poured out on us abundantly through Jesus Christ our Savior, that having been justified by His grace we should become heirs according to the hope of eternal life" (Titus 3:5-7).

To think that we add to Christ's sinless sacrifice is to cheapen it. It brings Him down and elevates us. Paul admonished, "For by grace you have been saved through faith, and that not of yourselves; it is the gift of God, not of works, lest anyone should boast" (Ephesians 2:8-9).

So, does that mean we should just live our lives however we want, and not try to do good? If you are asking that question, then you are missing the point. When you truly comprehend how wretched you are, and what Jesus did for you, it should stir a desire in you to do good and follow after Him. It's not that we are trying to work our way to Heaven. It is that we are trying to pattern our lives after our Savior. It is my prayer that as you deepen your faith, you will be on guard against this works righteousness attitude. Humble yourself, and remember who you are — and remember who He is. "For God so loved the world that He gave His only begotten Son" (John 3:16).

Verses for Further Study

Isaiah 64:6	Acts 4:12	Titus 3:5-7
Romans 3:10, 23	John 3:16; 14:6	Ephesians 2:8-9

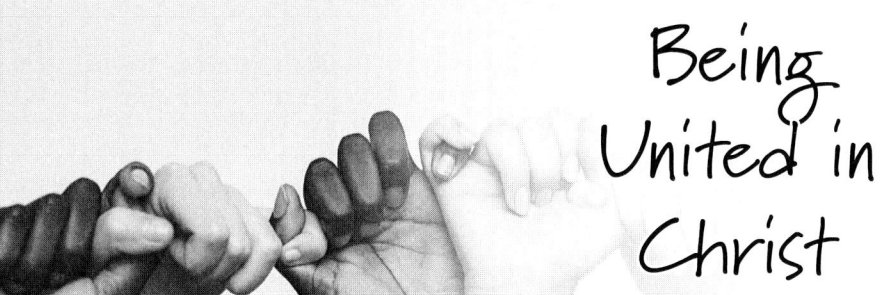

Being United in Christ

In John 17, Jesus prayed for unity. He boldly requested, "that they all may be one, as You, Father, are in Me, and I in You; that they also may be one in Us, that the world may believe that You sent Me" (John 17:21). Likewise, Paul wrote, "And He Himself gave some to be apostles, some prophets, some evangelists, and some pastors and teachers, for the equipping of the saints for the work of ministry, for the edifying of the body of Christ, till we all come to the unity of the faith and of the knowledge of the Son of God, to a perfect man, to the measure of the stature of the fullness of Christ" (Ephesians 4:11-13).

An honest evaluation of Christianity in America reveals that most congregations do not expend very much energy at all on unity. We hide under the umbrella of "autonomous congregations," rarely doing anything with congregations who are, in many cases, less than ten miles down the road. Sure, we will post flyers of area gospel meetings on a bulletin board, but when it comes to actually doing things together we leave that to our area wide youth devotionals.

Here's what I intend on teaching my children about being united in Christ.

There is no doubt in my mind that we have missed the mark on this one. In modern times, it is usually a big deal if 2-3 congregations go in together to hold a meeting or special community seminar. Oftentimes we don't get together to worship or sing together. Instead, most congregations spend lots of energy judging neighboring congregations. While we may never say it aloud, the truth is most Christians believe their congregation (and probably only their congregation) is doing things right—and all other congregations are suspect. After all, we reason that if members at neighboring congregations wanted to worship correctly then they would attend with us at our home congregation. Instead of uniting, what we've actually done is build walls.

79

Being United in Christ • Church Life

I challenge you to help tear down some of these walls during your lifetime. Yes, there may be congregations down the street that do things a little differently. However, if they are adhering to God's Word, then those matters of opinion must be viewed as simply that—matters of opinion. Understand; I am not suggesting you throw out doctrine to simply be united to everyone. The problem is often that we stop looking at Christ, and instead focus on men and circle ourselves around specific groups (see 1 Corinthians 1:10-16).

When Jesus was asked what is the greatest command, He replied, "You shall love the Lord your God with all your heart, with all your soul, and with all your mind." This is the first and greatest commandment. And the second is like it: "You shall love your neighbor as yourself" (Matthew 22:37-39). Notice this—we are commanded to love our neighbor as ourself. That is the second command.

Unity is a concept that is observed all the way back in the beginning of creation. Man was able to experience

What can you do to promote unity in all the areas of your life?

a unity with God in the Garden of Eden (Genesis 1-3). Sin shattered that unity and Jesus Christ was sent as the redeemer to help man be unified with God once again. We see unity playing a role in God's will, in the church, and ultimately where we will spend eternity. So let me encourage you to look around and ask yourself— how can we become more united with other Christians together? As you meditate on that, consider a few highlights from God's Word:

1 Peter 3:8 ESV "Finally, all of you, have unity of mind, sympathy, brotherly love, a tender heart, and a humble mind."

1 Corinthians 1:10 ESV "I appeal to you, brothers, by the name of our Lord Jesus Christ, that all of you agree, and that there be no divisions among you, but that you be united in the same mind and the same judgment."

2 Corinthians 13:11 ESV "Finally, brothers, rejoice. Aim for restoration, comfort one another, agree with one another, live in peace; and the God of love and peace will be with you."

Romans 12:4-5 ESV "For as in one body we have many members, and the members do not all have the same function, so we, though many, are one body in Christ, and individually members one of another."

Ephesians 4:1-6 ESV "I therefore, a prisoner for the Lord, urge you to walk in a manner worthy of the calling to which you have been called, with all humility and gentleness, with patience, bearing with one another in love, eager to maintain the unity of the Spirit in the bond of peace. There is one body and one Spirit just as you were called to the one hope that belongs to your call— one Lord, one faith, one baptism,"

Psalm 133:1 ESV "Behold, how good and pleasant it is when brothers dwell in unity!"

Romans 14:19 ESV "So then let us pursue what makes for peace and for mutual upbuilding."

Romans 12:16 ESV "Live in harmony with one another. Do not be haughty, but associate with the lowly. Never be wise in your own sight."

Ephesians 4:13 ESV "Until we all attain to the unity of the faith and of the knowledge of the Son of God, to mature manhood, to the measure of the stature of the fullness of Christ."

Romans 15:5-6 ESV "May the God of endurance and encouragement grant you to live in such harmony with one another, in accord with Christ Jesus. That together you may with one voice glorify the God and Father of our Lord Jesus Christ."

Philippians 2:2-3 ESV "Complete my joy by being of the same mind, having the same love, being in full accord and of one mind. Do nothing from rivalry or conceit, but in humility count others more significant than yourselves."

1 Corinthians 12:12 ESV "For just as the body is one and has many members, and all the members of the body, though many, are one body, so it is with Christ."

Amos 3:3 ESV "Do two walk together, unless they have agreed to meet?"

Satan is working hard at making sure Christians do not unite in our battle against him. Rather than uniting as a single, loud voice condemning things like abortion or same-sex marriage, we stay almost reclusive in our own buildings, hesitant to associate with neighboring congregations. Be a leader and set the example. Show fellow Christians the benefits of being united and keep a careful eye out for causes of disunity.

Verses for Further Study

John 17	2 Corinthians 13:11
Ephesians 4:1-6, 11-13	Romans 12; 14:19; 15:5-6
1 Corinthians 1:10-16; 12:12	Psalm 133:1
Matthew 22:37-39	Philippians 2:2-3
Genesis 1-3	Amos 3:3
1 Peter 3:8	

Being United in Christ • Church Life

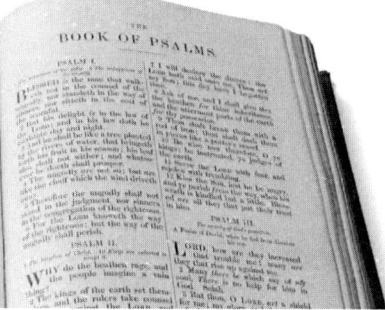

How We Got the Bible

It is becoming more and more common to meet individuals who were once faithful Christians but have now adopted a world view of skepticism and atheism. Having studied with dozens of these individuals, it has become painfully clear that they place absolutely no confidence in God's Word. They believe it was a book that has mistakes or was written by men, but they do not hold that it is inspired. Even many Christian parents remain silent when questioned by their children about how the Bible came into being.

Here's what I intend to teach my children regarding how we got the Bible.

Many skeptics claim that the Bible is a relatively recent document, as mankind did not possess the capability for written language until just a few thousand years ago. However, archeological evidence proves that writing was well established long before the beginning of the Hebrew nation. In fact, inscriptions found in ancient Babylon date back more than four thousand years. The importance of this should not be overlooked. Some would like to claim writing was not around when Moses walked the earth, yet evidence proves otherwise. Ancient people used many kinds of material for writing purposes; the Bible actually makes mention of a number of these materials:

Stone • Clay • Leather • Papyrus • Vellum or Parchment

Some skeptics would like to claim writing was not around when Moses walked the earth, yet evidence proves otherwise. Consider what we find in the pages of God's Word regarding how the written word has been passed down.

• **Stone** is the substance upon which the earliest writing in the Bible is found. Biblical examples of writing on stone can be found in Exodus 31:18; 34:1, 28; Deuteronomy 27:2-3; and Joshua 8:30-32.

• **Clay** was the predominant material for writing in Assyria and

Babylonia. This type of preservation of writing is what is referred to in Ezekiel 4:1: "You also, son of man, take a clay tablet and lay it before you, and portray on it a city, Jerusalem."

• **Leather** is not mentioned specifically in the Bible, though it was undoubtedly the material used for writing by the Hebrews. A scribe's knife, used for the purpose of erasures, is mentioned in Jeremiah 36:23. The Jewish Talmud, a code of traditional laws, explicitly called for the Scriptures to be copied on animal skins.

• **Papyrus** was the most widely used material for writing in the Grecian/Roman culture, though the Egyptians used it as far back as 2500 B.C.

• **Vellum or Parchment** came into prominence as a writing material due to the desire to build a worldwide library. No doubt, this was the material Paul requested Timothy to bring him in 2 Timothy 4:13. This material, made from the skins of animals but not tanned into leather, became the material upon which copies of the New Testament were made for about 1,000 years. Remember, the Bible was not written on a single occasion by a single author, but rather by a multitude of men over 1,600 years through gradual stages of growth.

Initially God's communication with man was oral. However, the time came when it was necessary for the divine will of God to be put in a permanent form. The Bible was written originally in three languages: Hebrew, Aramaic, and Greek. Scholars agree that almost all of the 39 Old Testament books were written in Hebrew (written backwards, right to left). Aramaic is a kindred language to Hebrew. (Nehemiah 8:8 suggests that the returned exiles did not understand pure Hebrew). The books comprising the New Testament were written in Greek, a "worldwide" language.

Until the invention of the printing press around 1450, the Bible had to be hand copied, word-for-word by scribes. These men took their jobs very seriously, counting letters and rows and destroying any copy that was deemed incorrect. Between the 7th and 11th century, groups of Jewish scribes known as Masoretes began to copy the Old Testament texts according to strict guidelines. The Masoretes maintained nearly perfect accuracy in their copies. It was the Masoretic manuscripts from which many versions of the Bible were translated.

Still, none of the original New Testament documents are in existence. But you don't need to hold an original to believe. (Have you ever held the "original" Constitution or original manuscripts of ancient books?) We only have copies of copies of copies. However, the discovery of the Dead Sea scrolls gives us confidence in what we read today! This circumstance has led skeptics to claim that we cannot

How We Got the Bible • Church Life

know whether we have the original Bible.

A God that can create the world can surely communicate His will to His creation. God knew that His Word would be preserved throughout history. Jesus declared, "Heaven and earth will pass away, but My Words will by no means pass away" (Matthew 24:35, see also Luke 21:33). The prophet Isaiah maintained, "The grass withers, the flower fades, But the Word of our God stands forever" (40:8). One can rest assured that the transmission and translation procedure is sufficiently stable for God's Word to be passed down to future generations by uninspired, imperfect translators. But how can we be sure what we read today is what the original writers penned?

We know how the original New Testament documents read because we have three surviving classes of **evidence** with which to reconstruct the original New Testament:
Greek manuscripts • Ancient versions • Patristic citations

The current number of Greek manuscript copies containing all or part of the New Testament is **5,745.** The official listing (as of 2007) of the several important categories of Greek New Testament manuscripts was put together by Bruce M. Metzger and can be summarized as follows:

Papyri ...118
Majuscule MSS ... 317
Minuscule MSS ... 2,877
Lectionary MSS ... 2,433
Total ... 5,745

Given that we have only a scant few manuscripts for other well known books, and their authenticity is not questioned, one wonders why the authenticity of the Bible — which boasts more than 5,000 manuscripts — is often questioned. Many will question; few will read it!

Verses for Further Study

Exodus 31:18; 34:1, 28	Ezekiel 4:1	Nehemiah 8:8
Deuteronomy 27:2-3	Jeremiah 36:23	Matthew 24:35
Joshua 8:30-32	2 Timothy 4:13	Luke 21:33, 40:8

How We Got the Bible • Church Life

Fasting

It has been said on more than one occasion that members of the church cannot get together without eating. In fact, some of my own seminars have been graded on the number of pounds I gained: "Well, that was a five pound meeting." We love to eat. We eat when we are happy and celebrating (birthdays, VBS, camp, anniversaries) and we eat when we are sad (deaths, sickness, hospital stays, or even breakups). Eating can bring comfort, allow for fellowship, and may even serve as a distraction.

Eating is a major part of our culture. We define our day around meals or what we are eating. And rare is the parent who has not heard hundreds of times: "What are we eating for dinner?" It is no surprise then that many pulpits remain silent on fasting — after all who wants to upset the applecart (unless those spilled apples could be put into a pie)? Preachers will readily joke about their stomachs being "chicken graveyards," but how many will touch on the Biblical topic of fasting?

Here's what I intend to teach my children regarding fasting.

I have a weakness for food. I love to eat good food. In fact, about the only thing I just won't eat is liver. Aside from that, I'm game to try just about anything. You know firsthand that I normally keep a stash of ice cream in the freezer, and it's not hard to talk me into stopping by a restaurant on the weekends. So understand what I'm about to share with you goes against my nature, and is something I have to work hard on.

The Bible records over twenty times this experience known as fasting (e.g., Jeremiah 36:6; Daniel 6:18; Daniel 9:3; Joel 2:12). Probably the most prominent example and most familiar passages come from Jesus. In Matthew chapter four, we find Jesus fasting when he is tempted by Satan. Just a few chapters later Jesus instructs:

Fasting • Church Life

85

"Moreover, when you fast, do not be like the hypocrites, with a sad countenance. For they disfigure their faces that they may appear to men to be **fasting**. Assuredly, I say to you, they have their reward" (Matthew 6:16).

In Matthew chapter nine, Jesus is questioned about his disciples and their fasting: "Then the disciples of John came to Him, saying, 'Why do we and the Pharisees fast often, but Your disciples do not fast?' And Jesus said to them, 'Can the friends of the bridegroom mourn as long as the bridegroom is with them? But the days will come when the bridegroom will be taken away from them, and **then they will fast**.'" (Matthew 9:14-15, emp. added).

So here is what we know. Jesus fasted. Jesus instructed us how to fast. And Jesus' disciples fasted. There are many more passages we could examine, but this is ample evidence that we should also be fasting.

Why? What is the purpose of fasting? Fasting is to make us more focused and more aware of our need for God. It is a temporary measure that reminds us that life is not about earthly pleasure, but rather there is a day coming when we will no longer need to fast! Fasting helps us to grow spiritually as we deny ourselves something in order to glorify and grow closer to God.

While Jesus does give some instruction in Matthew chapter six on fasting, He does not indicate things like how often or specifics on how. Many individuals try to jump in and do day-long (or even week-long) fasts having never fasted before. These individuals are setting themselves up for failure.

Let me recommend you start out purposefully fasting through a single meal. Then increase it to that same meal two or three days in a row. After that try fasting for an entire day. Many scholars recommend continuing to drink water (so you don't become dehydrated) and others recommend doing a juice fast — which would cut out solid foods, but would still give you some nutrients and sugars to give you enough strength to continue on throughout the day.

My recommendation is you start out small and increase from there. Be very conscientious of how your fasting causes you to treat others (in other words, it does no good to fast to get closer to God if you are grumpy all day with your siblings and parents!). And plan ahead! How will you deal with those times when you get really hungry? Will you use this time to read your Bible, take a walk outside, pray, etc.?

Fasting is not something I've perfected. But it is something that is in the Bible and we should work on. I'll make you a deal: you encourage me when I'm fasting, and I'll do my best not to put my big bowl of ice cream in front of you when you are fasting. Keep growing and keep studying.

Verses for Further Study

| Jeremiah 36:6 | Daniel 9:3 | Matthew 6:16 |
| Daniel 6:18 | Joel 2:12 | Matthew 9:14-15 |

Fasting • Church Life

Serve Him: Now!

I have been a Christian for several decades now, and I still struggle with an observation that I see throughout the church. Allow me to explain. When children reach fourteen or fifteen years of age, parents collectively hold their breath until those children make the decision to obey the Gospel and be baptized. Afterwards, there is rejoicing as Mom and Dad breathe a sigh of relief. Cards are sent. Prayers are offered. And we may even allow the newly converted male children to wait on the Lord's Table. But after a few weeks/months, that young person's zeal wanes, and we all return back to the "normal" activities of life. We don't expect much from this new Christian. In fact, truth be told, we don't expect anything except for them to continue attending services. After all, they have demands at school and will soon be heading off to college.

It is like baptism is their "cape" that will get them into heaven, and as long as they have that somewhere nearby, then that's enough. And so, our young people get into the habit of obtaining their cape and then promptly hanging it on a nearby coat rack. Surely we don't expect them to fly right away ... right? It's like we baptize our children and then put it on cruise control until we once again collectively hold our breath to see if they escaped college with their faith intact. Why have we allowed this to be the normal? This is not the pattern we find in the New Testament—so why is this the pattern we find in the church?

Here's what I intend to teach my children regarding putting off your service to Christ.

Once you make the decision to follow Christ, that becomes your lifelong commitment. It doesn't officially start once school is out or at a more convenient time. Rather, your decision to step onto the narrow path begins once you put on that new man (Colossians 3:8-10).

Saul (who would later become known as Paul) was persecuting Christians. He was a dangerous man for Christians to be around.

In Acts chapter 9, we find Saul's conversion and baptism. Saul went three days without food and water (verse 9), and then Ananias came to him and taught him the Truth. We then learn "So when he had received food, he was strengthened. Then Saul spent some days with the disciples at Damascus. **Immediately he preached the Christ in the synagogues, that He is the Son of God**" (Acts 9:19-20, emp. added). Saul didn't wait years and years to begin bearing fruit. The text says "immediately" he preached Christ! This is a man who was radically changed and wanted to tell the world about Jesus Christ. He was not interested in waiting a few years or waiting until he was out of college. He wanted to tell the lost about Jesus.

My prayer is that you will have Saul/Paul's attitude—that you will immediately look for opportunities to teach the Truth and bear fruit. Don't buy into what the world is promoting, that you don't start life until you are out of school. You are already alive, and you were created for good works (Ephesians 2:10)! God has blessed each of you with talents. Look for ways to use those talents for Him.

If you take the world's mentality of waiting until you are older then several things are likely to happen: (1) you will become cold and apathetic; (2) you will waste several years that you could have reached lost souls; (3) you will help perpetuate this false notion that only older people can bear fruit for Him; and (4) you will lose sight of the importance Christ should have in your life!

Don't wait. Come out of that water looking for ways to serve Him. Turn the world upside down, and don't let anyone tell you that you can't! After all, you are a new man with God on your side.

Family Challange

MAKE A LIST OF PEOPLE YOU WANT TO SHARE CHRIST WITH. AT THE END OF THE MONTH, SHARE YOUR RESULTS.

Verses for Further Study

| Colossians 3:8-10 | Acts 9:19-20 | Ephesians 2:10 |

Serve Him: NOW! • Church Life

Persecution

How much time do you spend aspiring toward happiness? How much time and energy do you spend avoiding persecution and trials? The vast majority of the population today considers the pursuit of happiness the "end-all" goal of their life. The "rat race" of life has millions of people trying to earn enough money so they can retire and hopefully have a carefree existence. We earnestly believe that if we work hard enough then we can avoid pain and sorrow.

The reality is vastly different from this empty pursuit. The reality is all people die. The reality is if you do not die suddenly from an accident then you will likely get sick or contract a disease. The reality is most individuals find themselves caring for their aging parents. The reality is most humans experience some type of pain and sorrow no matter how much money they have or whether they have reached retirement.

Unfortunately, many of our pulpits reinforce this notion of happiness being the goal. Sermons have been tweaked to tickle the ears of listeners and make them feel comfortable. Many preachers believe that all sermons should be "positive" in nature. Many elders want "feel good" sermons in an effort to retain or increase their "numbers." Sadly, this is not the prescription given by God's Word.

Here's what I intend to teach my children about persecution.

Life is hard. Your goal should not be to make it easy. Your goal should be to serve the Lord. Persecution is a stark reality about living the Christian life. "Yes, and all who desire to live godly in Christ Jesus will suffer persecution" (2 Timothy 3:12).

In John 15:20 we read Jesus admonishing, " Remember the word that I said to you, 'A servant is not greater than his master.' If they persecuted Me, they will also persecute you." James says to "count it

90

all joy when you fall into various trials, knowing that the testing of your faith produces patience" (James 1:2-3). Jesus observed, "Blessed are those who are persecuted for righteousness' sake, for theirs is the kingdom of heaven" (Matthew 5:10).

As crazy as it sounds, I hope you suffer persecution during your lifetime, because if you do not have to endure persecution then you probably are not living a life fully for Him. My job is not to train you to escape persecution, but rather my job is to teach you how to "stand" and recognize the value of persecution. James says we should count persecution as a joy—because it helps produce patience and further strengthens our faith.

I'll be honest with you—I don't like persecution. But I am now old enough to see the value in it. In fact, if my life goes too long without persecution I sometimes wonder if I am standing strong enough for Him. Am I truly defending God's Word? Never forget that the darkness does not like the light. If we are truly being a light to the dark world around us we will be persecuted.

If you are around people or pulpits that are espousing our goal is to be happy and have an easy life I hope you will remember this letter. I hope a red flag will go up in your mind and you will see that this goal is contrary to God's Word. Happiness and an easy life are not wrong, but they should not be your goals. You goals are to get to heaven and to take as many people with you as you can.

Verses for Further Study

2 Timothy 3:12	James 1:2-3
John 15:20	Matthew 5:10

Persecution • Church Life

This Hurts Me A Lot More Than It Hurts You

Methods of child discipline "evolve" as our culture continues to change and drift. Popular books and trends have a way of setting a standard that can last for two or three generations. For instance, many of today's grandparents can remember Dr. Spock's Baby and Childcare and his advice on how to rear children. The concept of "time out" really took root during my generation—a concept that was completely foreign to our grandparents. Ironically, this is a topic that affects everyone but that is rarely discussed.

It is no secret that discipline has become much more lax in the past few decades. Corporal punishment has almost gone the way of the dinosaur in most school systems. I doubt the average parent has any idea the amount of red tape and paperwork involved in administering a spanking in public schools today. Under the guise of "love" and anti-abuse, many areas of the world have already outlawed spanking. This anti-spanking trend appears to be gaining ground and picking up speed.

Public pressure has all but silenced Christians. Many Christians now find themselves worried that any public display of discipline may resort in Child Protective Services removing their children from the home. To compound the problem, pulpits have stopped preaching specifics in this area and are now content to suggest vague generalities. We will readily condemn homosexuals and atheists, but we have forgotten that Paul put those who are disobedient to parents into the same chapter as the homosexuals and haters of God (Romans 1:28-30).

Here's what I intend to teach my children about discipline.

I will likely never forget the occasion in which I had to get you all out of bed and "line you all up" to administer a spanking. (And I suspect you might not forget it as well.) Earlier in the day, I had mentioned that there would be a punishment if you all did not do something your mom

92

and I had requested. During my nightly check of the house, I realized that what we requested had gone undone. You will likely never know how badly I wanted to just do it myself and go on. It would have been so quick and easy. But I knew I couldn't. I loved you too much. And so through sobs and tears, I spanked each one of you—as a reminder to be obedient.

You know we believe in spanking. Each one of you has felt the swats and seen the dreaded "wooden spoon." The concept of "time out" is kind of a joke in our household. I have told you on more than one occasion that if my parents had put me in time out, I would have simply used that time to figure out how not to get caught the next time! We have tried to convey discipline in a Biblical fashion, and have worked hard not to ever punish you in anger. While this may be hard to understand, we spank you because we love you dearly and want you to go to Heaven! That is why I try to remember to tell you I love you and why I am disciplining you when the need arises.

Spanking is a forgotten tool in modern times. Many people are afraid that it might be abusive or scar children emotionally. And if done wrongly like out of anger it can. However, your mom and I believe the Bible is a lot smarter than any "self-help" book or current trend. Solomon in his wisdom declared, "He who spares his rod hates his son, but he who loves him disciplines him promptly" (Proverbs 13:24). Later on he cautioned, "Do not withhold correction from a child, for if you beat him with a rod, he will not die. You shall beat him with a rod and deliver his soul from hell" (Proverbs 23:13-14). I have listened to many Bible "scholars" try to put a different spin on these verses, suggesting that it is not actually talking about spanking children. These are the same people who fight hard to defend other Truths found in God's Word. Those verses are not hard to understand, and they don't change over time. (Consider also Proverbs 22:15).

Solomon warned, "Chasten your son while there is hope, and do not set your heart on his destruction (Proverbs 19:18). Now contrast that with a statement he wrote earlier: "My son, do not despise the chastening of the Lord, nor detest his correction; for whom the Lord loves He corrects, just as a father the son in whom he delights" (Proverbs 3:11-12). My prayer is that one day the relationship and discipline you have learned from me will be transferred into your relationship with your Heavenly Father.

On a few occasions you have heard your parents say, "Their parents must not love them as much as we love you" when discussing what someone else "gets away with" or poor behavior. While this may not

93

make logical sense now, in time I guarantee it will. During your life you will see countless examples of young people who have ruined their lives in folly. They are literally bringing shame to their parents. The Proverb writer noted: "The rod and rebuke give wisdom, but a child left to himself brings shame to his mother" (29:15).

Thankfully, we have entered a stage in life where spanking has tapered off. God's way works! The Bible told us, "Correct your son, and he will give you rest; yes, he will give delight to your soul (Proverbs 29:17). I am thankful that your obedience is now giving us delight. I pray you will reflect back and choose God's way for your children one day.

Verses for Further Study

Romans 1:28-30   Proverbs 3:11-12; 13:24; 19:18; 22:15; 23:13-14; 29:15, 17

Discipline

We ought to be ashamed—but we are not. Children today are running around knocking people over in church auditoriums, and almost nobody says a word. Sadly, when you do try to correct the child's misbehavior they will either smart off back to you or his or her parent will get mad and defend the misbehaving child. Before the final "Amen" has been said children will be talking to their parents like dogs if they are not getting their way about where the family is eating out for lunch. And sadly, instead of correcting bad behavior today's parents make excuses for their children saying, "They stayed up too late and are tired" or "He has ADHD and hasn't taken his medicine."

Before I get barraged with emails and hate-filled correspondence, please understand that I know that some children really do suffer from ADHD and need medication—and I am thankful medications exist for those children. However, I also know many children are diagnosed with this condition who simply receive no discipline in the home and have never been trained to behave. I've heard many older Christians point out that this condition did not exist when they were young and instead of popping pills, parents and teachers would pop rear-ends.

What happened to parenting? What happened to correcting bad behavior? With both parents working outside the home in many families, children often times are left raising themselves and parents are reluctant to discipline a child when they come home from a long day at work. The Bible speaks clearly about what happens when a child is left to himself (Proverbs 29:15). Instead of parenting, children are seeing therapists, counselors, chiropractors, and taking prescriptions in an effort to fix the problem. Maybe the problem lies in the heart of the child, and the real solution is two parents who will dare to discipline properly.

Here's what I intend to teach my children regarding discipline.

95

I've heard countless stories from older Christians—stories of how their parents made them go out to a specific tree when they were little and bring in a small branch that would be used on their backside. I've heard stories of people putting on extra layers of underwear, people hiding Dad's belt so he couldn't find it, moms carrying wooden spoons around in their purse. Every single time I hear these stories—and I've heard a lot of them—they are always told with a smile, and sometimes with a hint of laughter as the person recounts what they had done. The writer of Hebrews wrote, "Now no chastening seems to be joyful for the present, but painful; nevertheless, afterward it yields the peaceable fruit of righteousness to those who have been trained by it" (Hebrews 12:11).

The Bible speaks plainly that parents are to discipline misbehaving children. Notice I said discipline and not abuse. The underlying reason that parents should discipline is love. "My son, do not despise the chastening of the Lord, nor be discouraged when you are rebuked by Him; For whom the Lord loves He chastens, and scourges every son whom He receives" (Hebrews 12:5-6; see also Revelation 3:19). "My son, do not despise the chastening of the Lord, nor detest His correction; For whom the Lord loves He corrects, just as a father the son in whom he delights" (Proverbs 3:11-12).

Many people have shared various "offenses" they did that resulted in discipline, but the one that usually tops the list is talking back to parents. It simply was not done in days gone by. I will sometimes share the very true story of me talking back to my dad—one time—at the dinner table. It hasn't happened again, and it won't. Solomon wrote, "He who spares his rod hates his son, but he who loves him disciplines him promptly" (Proverbs 13:24). Today, it is not uncommon to hear children talking back to parents or teachers. After all, they know they will not receive any type of discipline for it.

Sadly, political correctness has ruined discipline in the home. Modern parents fear injuring a child's self-esteem and so they allow the children to misbehave or talk in a disrespectful manner. Discipline has turned into things like "time-out" and positive behavior modification. While these new methods may lead to short-term compliance, the bottom line is the real lesson is not learned and the child falls into the same misbehaving pattern time and time again. Solomon wisely wrote, "Do not withhold correction from a child, for if you beat him with a rod, he will not die. You shall beat him with a rod, and deliver his soul from hell" (Proverbs 23:12-14).

Just how serious is it when children misbehave? Well consider the list Paul gives of behaviors that are not fitting to God (Romans 1:28). In the list that follows he mentions things like haters of God, murderers, violent, proud, and ... children that disobey their parents. It's important to God that children obey—because after all, if they won't obey their earthly father then they will grow up to disobey their heavenly Father. Think about it ...

Verses for Further Study

Hebrews 12: 5-6, 11	Prov. 3:11-12;13:24; 23:12-14; 29:15
Revelation 3:19	Romans 1:28

Discipline • Parenting

Adoption

It has become such a "standard" that newly married couples often brace themselves for the questions, having only been wed for a few mere months: "When will you all have children?" Oh, there are variations of the question, but it boils down to this: You've now been married for a while, and our culture has determined that the next step is a child—so when will you be bringing one home?

For many people this is nothing more than friendly banter – for instance, parents wanting grandchildren. But for other couples, these words sting and cause an unrelenting string of emotions — as these couples find themselves unable to conceive. Married couples are "expected" to have children, so what happens when those expectations are not forthcoming?

For many, it means drugs to help with ovulation. For others, it means trips to fertility clinics for expensive procedures, such as artificial insemination or in vitro fertilization. Rarely do we stop and ask if these procedures are ethically right in the eyes of God — all we know is we want a child and this clinic has given us great odds.

Rare is the elder or preacher who will teach about modern fertility practices, and as such, many Christians plunge blindly forward, only to discover that they have created 12-15 healthy living embryos that must now be "stored" (frozen) or "discarded" (killed). But there is another alternative — a beautiful alternative on which Christians should be informed.

Here's what I intend to teach my children on the topic of adoption.

Children are special; however, I want you to know that while our culture expects couples to have children, you can be a faithful servant of God without having children. If, however, you choose to pursue parenthood, I want to make sure:

98

(1) You do it without violating the marriage bed or killing embryos.

(2) You do it for the right purpose.

Adoption is a beautiful choice. The Bible is replete with passages regarding how Christians should take care of two special groups — widows and orphans (James 1:27; see also Exodus 22:22-23). However, take care that you adopt a child for the right reason.

Voddie Baucom is a Baptist preacher who has adopted children. He gives several warnings to parents who are considering the process. For instance, he encouraged parents not to adopt a child simply to fill a void in your lives. Understand that God must be first and foremost, thus He should fill that void. Otherwise, if you try to fill it with a child (or golf, shopping, etc.) you risk committing the sin of idolatry, putting something ahead of God.

Do not adopt a child to try and match someone who looks like you to fix your broken mental image of what your family "was supposed" to look like. If you follow this path you are simply trying to fix this self-centered image of "family," rather than bringing a child into your home for the right reason.

Do not adopt a child because you think your life will be incomplete without a child. Many righteous people have served God faithfully without ever parenting a child. Also do not adopt a child simply to share your wealth and ease your conscience.

Never forget there are things in life worse than being poor, such as being spiritually lost. And, finally, do not adopt a child thinking you are doing a good deed, trying to earn God's favor.

Rearing children—whether adopted or not—should be about returning those children to God. If you open your home to children, it must be with the understanding that it has nothing to do with their previous heritage or culture, but rather it has everything to do with getting those children to Heaven and loving them.

Why is this such a big deal? Because earthly adoption should mirror the vertical adoption we read about in the Bible. Look closely at Ephesians 1:3-6. Listen carefully to what Paul wrote to the church in Galatia: "God sent forth His Son, born of a woman, born under the law, to redeem those who were under the law, that we might receive the adoption as sons. And because you are sons ..." (Galatians 4:4-6). Our vertical adoption from God did not come with conditions. It did not happen because of our skin color or gender. God has adopted us because of His incredible love for us, and by doing so we are now His children with no qualifiers about our past heritage. Likewise, our earthly adoptions should mimic this. An earthly or horizontal adoption is a small picture of God's vertical adoption. It's not about race, socio-economic status, gender, hair color, eye color—but rather, it is about blessing a child with the knowledge of Jesus Christ, and returning those precious children to Him.

Do not allow society to steer you. Rearing children is a huge responsibility, but a gift that has so many rewards. If you want children and are unable to conceive, then consider adoption—because there are many precious souls that need a loving home and need to learn about Him.

Verses for Further Study

James 1:27	Ephesians 1:3- 6
Exodus 22:22-23	Galatians 4:4-6

Adoption • Parenting

Sexual Abuse/ Sexual Predators

My childhood was fairly "sweet and innocent." I was picked on by my older brothers, loved by my parents, and usually had a friendly pet dog somewhere close by. Oh, there was the occasional run-in with neighborhood bullies or the occasional dirty joke passed around on the school bus. But over all, my childhood years were pretty innocent.

I grew up in a home in a time where we were taught to respect teachers, police officers, and adults in general. Older people were individuals who you could always turn to if you were lost, hurt, or needed a hand. I still remember the first time the "blinds" were lifted from my innocence, and I learned of a Christian adult who had done something very inappropriate. Up until that point, I had never feared getting hugs in church or being patted by older people. With one fell swoop, my innocent world quickly changed.

We don't talk about child abuse in the church... and shame on us because in many cases the church building has become a place in which adults prey on children. I suspect elders don't want something so distasteful mentioned from the pulpit, and preachers wrestle with how to communicate the problem while protecting innocent ears. Also, many preachers and elders have chosen to leave that discussion to the home—not realizing that many victims come from broken homes in which those conversations never take place. Given the hyper-sexualization of our culture and given the numerous accounts of pedophilia in the news, this is a topic we must address.

Here is what I intend on telling my children about sexual predators.

Until you experience parenthood, you will never truly know the sense of protection that your mother and I share for your well being. We want to keep you safe, even if it means we must sacrifice our own lives. In order to do that, we must be very diligent. More than anything we want you safe—but there may be times we need your help!

I wish that I could tell you that everyone in the world is good. But the reality is that we live in a world that has "fallen" since the time of Adam and Eve, and there are people out there who, if given the chance, might try to hurt you. So what should you do if one of these individuals comes to you? Run and tell me or your mom immediately.

During the time of Noah, we learn that men's thoughts were on evil continually (Genesis 6:5). Thankfully, we live in a time that has not gotten that bad. However, as we have taught you, there are many individuals who are filling their minds with bad material instead of wholesome material (see Romans 1:28-32). That bad material may make them want to do things they shouldn't to little children.

We have taught you since you were little that there are some places on your body that only mommies and daddies (or future spouses) should see (or doctors, with your parents present). If anyone ever tries to touch those places, or asks you to touch them in those places, run away and tell us immediately. I assure you we will not be mad. Even if they tell you that it is okay, run away or yell, "You are not my mommy or daddy!" These individuals are suffering from a type of sickness and they need help.

The hard part in our task is these people won't be wearing an ugly black cape or have horns on their heads. They will look just like normal adults — people you see every day. Some of these individuals may live in our neighborhood, some may worship with us at church, and some may even come into our home. If someone ever tries to get you into a room by yourself, tell them no or tell them you want your parents to come with you. Yell out "You are not my mommy!"

So here's our job. I want you to imagine those areas of your body as a massive steel door like on a bank vault. No one gets the key except your future mate. Those areas of your body are special, and God meant for them to be seen only by parents caring for small children or by spouses. As you grow older we can talk more about why people might do this or why God created those special places. But for now our job is to keep that vault door shut no matter who wants to open it! It is never okay for adults to look at you there or touch you there—even if you know the person. This is one of those letters I wish I never had to write. But unfortunately I do. I write it with tears and love.

Verses for Further Study

Genesis 6:5   Romans 1:28-32

Legacy

Walk through any cemetery and glance at the dates that surround you. Many tombstones speak of an individual who lived before computers, cars, or indoor plumbing existed. In my hometown of Franklin, Tennessee, we have a cemetery in which many soldiers from the Civil War are buried. Many of these soldiers have been dead for close to 150 years. Consider for a moment that aside from these pieces of granite or marble, there are relatively few "material" possessions from these soldiers still in existence. So what did these men of previous generations leave behind? Simply put, every single one of them left behind some type of legacy.

Americans spend an enormous amount of time amassing "material" things—so we certainly don't like to think about the very real fact that one day, all of it will be gone. Our cars will rust and probably be recycled into future material. Our homes will decay and one day be replaced. Our stocks, clothes, and electronics will be things of the past. The only thing that will be passed into the future will be our legacy. While we draft up wills in consideration of where our earthly possessions will go, we don't give much thought about passing along a living legacy.

Here's what I intend to teach my children on their legacy.

When I die, each one of you will receive some of my physical possessions. While I hope those goods help you in your future walks of life, my prayer is that you will treasure the spiritual training that your mom and I passed on even more than the material things. I have shared with each of you that my greatest desire is to see you in Heaven—for you to marry strong Christians and rear future generations of Christians. For you see, this will be my legacy. This is what I will be passing down to generations I will never live to see.

Consider how it would feel if you knew someone back in 1912 was working diligently to make sure you remained faithful to God. That is

Legacy • Parenting

103

a unique feeling and one you may struggle to truly grasp. My prayer is that you will look into the future and consider what you can do to ensure future generations of Harrubs will be faithful. The reality is in 100 years people will not care what your career was—and more than likely you will be forgotten. But your grandchildren and great-grandchildren will still be affecting the world. Start thinking now about what your legacy will be. Maybe for you it will be 100 years of no unfaithfulness to God in your lineage. Or maybe your legacy will be 100 years without divorce or alcoholic beverages. The point is you need to consider what your legacy will be, and then start working diligently, with passion and perseverance, toward that goal (Proverbs 16:3).

One of the greatest blessings in the Bible was given to a family that held to a family legacy of no alcoholic beverages. In Jeremiah 35 we learn about the Rechabites. The Rechabites were the descendants of Rechab through Jonadab (or Jehonadab). This special family belonged to the Kenites who accompanied the children of Israel into the Promised Land and dwelt among them. We know for instance Moses married a Kenite wife (Judges 1:16).

In Jeremiah 35 the descendants of Jonadab are offered wine. We find their response in verse 6: "But they said, 'We will drink no wine, for Jonadab the son of Rechab, our father, commanded us, saying, "You shall drink no wine, you nor your sons, forever."' Because of their obedience, this family receives one of the strongest blessings in the Bible.

And Jeremiah said to the house of the Rechabites, "Thus says the Lord of hosts, the God of Israel: 'Because you have obeyed the commandment of Jonadab your father, and kept all his precepts and done according to all that he commanded you,' therefore thus says the Lord of hosts, the God of Israel: 'Jonadab the son of Rechab **shall not lack a man to stand before Me forever'"** (Jeremiah 35:18-19, emp. added).

My children, this is a legacy! This blessing is worth far more than any material possession I can pass along to you. The reality is we will all leave behind a legacy. I pray that your legacy will be seen through future generations of faithful Christians. Always remember Judges 2:10, "When all that generation had been gathered to their fathers, another generation arose after them who did not know the Lord nor the work which He had done for Israel." Hopefully your children will grow to be future elders, preachers, and Christian homemakers. Consider the words of the inspired psalmist: "The words of the Lord are pure words, like silver tried in a furnace of earth, purified seven times. You shall keep them, O Lord, You shall preserve them from this generation forever" (Psalm 12:6-7). Now if we can just figure out who gets my collection of ball caps when I'm gone.

Family Discussion

WHAT KIND OF LEGACY DO YOU WANT TO LEAVE FOR YOUR CHILDREN? WHAT ABOUT YOUR GRANDCHILDREN?

HOW WILL YOU GO ABOUT LEAVING THAT LEGACY? WHAT PLANS DO YOU NEED TO MAKE TO ENSURE THAT IT HAPPENS?

Verses for Further Study

Proverbs 16:3	Jeremiah 35:6, 18-19
Judges 1:16; 2:10	Psalm 12:6-7

Legacy • Parenting

Socialization

I have heard the question too many times to count. Normally parents who are considering alternative ways to educate their children pose the question. However, it has come from grandparents, elders, and even preachers: "Aren't you worried about socialization?"

I used to get a little upset when this question was posed, because it was often asked like I was withholding an essential "vitamin" from my children that would stunt their growth and development. It was usually posed in a way that questioned my ability to parent. Today I just laugh.

Even though we are called to be different from the world (Romans 12:1-2), our current Christian culture is convinced Christian young people should spend a great deal of time "socializing" with people their own age. The social skills of anyone who does not attend public schools or is not involved in group activities like sports teams, band, clubs, etc. is questioned.

It's no secret that there have been homeschoolers who have come across as socially awkward. However, to label all children that are not enrolled in public school as socially inept is a gross generalization. (I might gently point out there are also public school students who come across as socially inept, not able to talk to adults and look them in the eye.)

And so, even in the church, the question comes: "Aren't you worried about socialization?"

Here's what I intend to teach my children regarding socialization.

We made a rule a long time ago that we would always welcome your friends over to our house whenever they are able to visit. There are many weeks I wonder if we should rethink that rule—because rarely does a week pass by that we don't have friends over 1-2 times per week.

106

Add to this, we spend countless hours on the road going to various church activities, visiting shut-ins, and attending sports activities. Mix into that the dozens of friends you have collected all over the world as we travel to "Origins" seminars, and you begin to understand why your mom and I don't worry about the "socialization" question. There are many times when I wish you were a little less social!

However, when it comes to socialization there are two important points I want to mention to you. When you look at the definition of socialize, one of the keys words that you will read is "society." Your mom and I don't want you to conform you to society. We don't want you just to be "social citizens." Our passion and life-long goal is for you to be warriors for Christ. Second, we don't just want to rear children who are comfortable talking to their own peer group. We love watching you interact with young and old alike.

God made man to be social. In fact, one of the cruelest forms of punishment we have come up with is isolation. It is important that you develop the skills to communicate with others around you. You can't live on an island or in a box. But just what kind of "socialization" are we really talking about?

I want to peel back the curtain and allow you to see what my mind thinks when someone asks me if we are worried about you being socialized.

My immediate thought these days is:
I don't want my children socialized into drugs and alcohol.
I don't want my children socialized into bad language.
I don't want my children socialized into disrespecting adults.
I don't want my children socialized into tattoos and piercings.
I don't want my children socialized into thinking siblings are lame.
I don't want my children socialized into thinking they should rebel against parents.
I don't want my children socialized into immodest clothing.
I don't want my children socialized into sexual activity.
I don't want my children socialized into ungodly music.
I don't want my children socialized into pornography.
I don't want my children socialized into an obsession of social media.
I don't want my children socialized into the modern dating scene.
I don't want my children socialized into things like prom and homecoming.

Life can be difficult sometimes. It is important to surround yourself

Socialization • Parenting

with friends you can laugh and cry with. When you "socialize," make sure it is with people who can help you get to Heaven. Paul's words are still very valid today: "Do not be deceived: 'Evil company corrupts good habits'" (1 Corinthians 15:33).

WHAT FORMS OF SOCIALIZATION CAN MEET YOUR NEEDS AND ALIGN WITH BIBLICAL PRINCIPLES?

Verse for Further Study
1 Corinthians 15:33

Socialization • Parenting

Bullying

Almost every month we read about a student who has taken his/her own life because they were bullied to the breaking point. The cruelty may take place in classrooms where young people are ridiculed for what they wear or how they look. Or it may take place online in the form of cyber bullying that goes viral. Often other young people will see what's happening and instead of putting a stop to it, they end up joining in – a 'pack' mentality in which these vicious wolves verbally shred their victim to pieces.

Bullying is a topic that is not often discussed in the church, even though many families are thrust into this dilemma. What do you tell a child who is the victim of such brutal behavior? Or what do parents of the 'bully' do to put a stop to this behavior?

Sadly, bullying does not stop when one graduates from high school. Even as adults there are those who continue this behavior – even in the church. So what is one to do?

Here's what I intend to teach my children regarding bullying.

Your mom and I try very hard to protect you from certain things in this world. However, there is one thing that may enter into the fortress we have built around you during your formative years – bullying. The sad fact of the matter is that kids can be mean (adults can too, for that matter!). I suspect everyone living has had at least one run-in with a bully. Both your mom and I remember individuals at school being mean and trying to push us around. You will probably experience this same anxiety and/or fear. So let's talk about what God would have you do.

The word bully is not found in God's Word. However, the words foolish, brutish, or stupid can be found (see Jude v. 10; Proverbs 12:1; Isaiah 19:11; Psalm 14:1). The word brute often comes from a Hebrew word that means "stupid or foolish beasts". These are animals that act foolishly without thinking – often in herds or packs, just like bullies. Pharaoh was an excellent Biblical example of a bully -- oppressing the Israelites and forcing them to work even harder under worse conditions. But remember, even though the Pharaoh thought he could get away with such cruel behavior, God was still in control.

Let me point out that bullying is a heart problem – and is sinful. Examine the things God hates in Proverbs 6:16-19 and you will see many of the same heart problems shared by bullies. Spend a moment comparing the heart of a bully versus the heart of a true Christian. If you are serious about being a servant of Christ, you will stay well away from this type of behavior. This includes being a part of 'the pack' of kids who cheer on bullies. Not only that, but if you want to be Christ-like, you will also extend a hand to others who may be bullied. We are to help the weak and

The word bully is not found in God's Word. However, the words foolish, brutish, or stupid can be found!

needy. This means you may have to go against the crowd on occasions and defend those who are being bullied – but that's part of what we do as Christians.

As hard as it may seem, we are to love those who are being mean to us – remember they have souls too! So our first defense is prayer. Make your petitions known to God. Second, we must consider our response and how it might influence those around us. Jesus said, 'But I say to you, love your enemies, bless those who curse you, do good to those who hate you, and pray for those who spitefully use you and persecute you, that you may be sons of your Father in heaven; for He makes His sun rise on the evil and on the good, and sends rain on the just and on the unjust' (Matthew 5:44-45). Work hard to be a Christian example – even to bullies.

Unfortunately, there may be times when the pain is unending. On those occasions, Jesus does not expect you to simply curl up into a ball and continue taking a beating. Instead, alert your mom or me, (or adults who may be present) and allow us to lend a hand. Part of my job as your father is to protect you. We see Biblical examples of men defending their families in the Bible. If the situation escalates to

110

the point that you are hurting, then please let someone know. We can help you through the situation, whether it means talking to the bully or his/her parents, or even removing you from the situation. While interactions with this bully may bring you to tears daily, never forget this phase in your life is temporary – you won't have to live your life surrounded by this individual forever! And never forget the God you serve is bigger than any bully you may face.

Questions

WHAT CAN YOU DO BEFORE SOMETHING HAPPENS TO MAKE SURE YOU RESPOND APPROPRIATELY TO BULLIES?

Bullying • Parenting

Verses for Further Study

Jude v. 10	Isaiah 19:11	Proverbs 6:16-19
Proverbs 12:1	Psalm 14:1	Matthew 5:44-45

Grandparents

There is a relationship that exists that I can't fully comprehend. Let me restate that—I can comprehend it, but only from one direction. That relationship is between a grandparent and a grandchild. Not having any grandchildren (yet), I can only speculate as what it feels like to have grandchildren.

It's not a stretch to say that most grandparents love to spoil their grandchildren. (I suspect it is a unique way of getting back at their children for all the gray hairs they added.) In years past, grandparents would carry wallets full of pictures of their grandchildren. If asked today, many grandparents grab their smartphone or iPad and begin to show a cascade of pictures of grandchildren from birth to present. Grandparents have even taken over social media sites like Facebook in an effort to keep up with grandchildren and distant friends.

We know grandparents love to give their grandchildren things — but what about the legacy they are leaving? What about how we are supposed to treat them?

Here's what I intend to teach my children about grandparents.

I still remember when my dad's father died. He was the first person I was close to that I knew who died. My mother's dad passed away before I was born, so "Papa" was the only grandfather I knew. I was young when he died (7 years old), and only possess a few memories of him. But his life and death taught me a great deal about our relatively short time here on earth. His death was a very real reminder that no one escapes death, and helped me in getting my priorities right. It was my grandfather who really helped me begin to understand what we sometimes refer to as the circle of life. While my dad received some of his physical possessions when Papa died, what was really handed down was the legacy of our family name. One day that legacy will be handed down to you.

You have been blessed to know all of your grandparents. These special people love you more than you can imagine, and they serve as a window into the past — they can help you understand your parents better. It is important to remember that life was different when they were growing up — different does not mean better or worse, just different (e.g., no computers or cell phones, but often closer families and more home-cooked meals). It is my hope that your relationship with your grandparents will teach you a lot, and be long-lasting. It is also my hope that you will never forget that if it were not for these individuals, you would not be here — so like all older individuals, they deserve your upmost respect. Honor them in your speech and actions (Leviticus 19:32; Psalm 71:9).

The Bible records over and over the importance of family relationships — and handing down our faith to future generations. In Deuteronomy 4:9 Moses admonished, "Only take heed to yourself, and diligently keep yourself, lest you forget the things your eyes have seen and lest they depart from your heart all the days of your life. And teach them to your children and grandchildren." Your grandparents play a role in teaching and instructing you. Learn from them—they often had to figure out things just by doing it (remember Google wasn't around!). Likewise, in 1 Timothy 5:4 we discover that you play a role in helping to care for them.

One of the most important lessons you will learn from your grandparents is the lesson of love. They loved you before you were even born — not because of something you did or how you look — but because of who you are. Additionally, I hope you will learn the lesson of family from your grandparents. The book of Genesis records over and over genealogies — focusing on the "seed" of specific families. By learning about your ancestors you can better appreciate what made you the person you are today and also paints a vision of our heritage back to the Flood and eventually Adam and Eve. So love your grandparents, spend time with them, and let them spoil you. But just remember, I will pay you back one day with your children ...

Verses for Further Study

Leviticus 19:32	Deuteronomy 4:9
Psalm 71:9	1 Timothy 5:4

113

Grandparents • Parenting

In-Laws

Countless volumes have been written about marriage and the importance of selecting a mate who will help you get to Heaven. But there is an aspect of this selection process that is often overlooked or simply joked about — in-laws.

Mothers-in-law are often on the receiving end of cruel jokes and are frequently portrayed in sitcoms or movies as wearisome. Don't let culture shape your beliefs about your in-laws. The reality is these individuals are the ones who helped mold and shape your future spouse. Through their actions and words they helped form the worldview and priorities of their children — so they play a vital role in the foundation of your marriage.

In the church, we often talk about the importance of marriage — an institution formed by God, and we also hear lessons about marrying faithful Christians. But rarely do we talk to young people about the importance of looking at the parents of potential mates.

Here's what I intend to teach my children regarding in-laws.

It has wisely been said many times, "You don't just marry the person, you also get the family as well." I want to preface what I'm about to say by telling you something that you already know — thankfully, I have wonderful in-laws whom I love very much. My prayer is that you will be blessed with the same.

The individuals who have likely influenced your spouse the most are his/her parents. In most cases, they will have spent eighteen years (or more) giving instruction and correction to your future mate. They have given them a picture of what "family" is all about. With this is mind, you would be foolish not to spend some time getting to know these individuals — learning what they value and why. Has your potential spouse grown up in a house that is centered on God and His Word, or is church just something they do? The answer to this question is extremely important.

Observe their marriage—keeping in mind this is what your future spouse views as "normal." Are they loving to one another? Do they help one another? How do they deal with conflict?

It is also useful observing the behavior between your potential mate and his/her parents. A young man who does not speak respectfully or treat his mother kindly says a great deal about the way he will treat his future spouse. Likewise, if a young man is kind and caring to his mother there is a good chance he will treat his future wife in a similar fashion.

I encourage you to also look at the relationship between your potential spouse and his or her parents. Do they communicate well and feel comfortable discussing anything, or do you find conversations tense and requiring lots of "work"? Are there "issues" that remained unresolved or cause anger? Remember these are the individuals who you will likely be spending a great number of holidays with in the future — and also the individuals who will serve as grandparents to your children.

And while you may not be thinking about it now, these are also the individuals you will be caring for as they age. Are these individuals you would feel comfortable with if they moved in when they are no longer able to care for themselves?

David is a textbook example of what happens when one marries with little regard to the in-laws. In 1 Samuel 18:17, we learn that Saul intended to give Merab, his oldest daughter, to David, but after time passed, she married Adriel the Meholathite. The text indicates that Michal, another of Saul's daughter's, loved David. And again, Saul viewed this relationship as a way to snare David, having him killed by the Philistines.

While most in-laws today do not plot to kill the spouse of their children, oftentimes they can kill them spiritually. The influence, beliefs, and priorities of in-laws should be greatly considered before committing to a marriage relationship. Had David considered the true character of his in-laws, he may have wisely chosen a different environment in which to begin his family. How many modern day marriages have crumbled as a result of in-laws whose different beliefs worked against the marriage relationship?

It is my prayer that your mother and I will be great in-laws for your potential mate — and we hope you end up with great in-laws as well. Take the time to invest in a relationship with your in-laws. The future benefits will be immeasurable.

Verse for Further Study
1 Samuel 18:17

In-Laws • Parenting

The Dinner Table

I was talking to a small group of people recently and realized that the American dinner table was going the way of the dinosaur. It's becoming rare for families to gather around the dinner table to eat and fellowship together. One individual told me that her family rarely ate together. The "dad" would eat in the living room watching television. Everyone else in the family would grab their meal and head off to separate rooms. I was very saddened and troubled to hear this.

The fact of the matter is families are too busy these days to gather around the table much. We eat on the go, often grabbing something at a local restaurant before heading off to football or band practice. Satan has convinced American Christians that we need to be involved in all kinds of activities. Unfortunately his lies are coming at the expense of the family. We are fractionated, hurried, and we really don't know one another as well any more.

This frantic pace has also affected relationships in the church. Rarely do Christians invite other families over for meals. Rarely do we sit around a dining room table just talking and sharing our thoughts and dreams. As a result, many Christians do not really know the other members in their local congregations. Probably the most common lie Christians utter is "I'm fine" when asked how we are doing in a church hallway. An honest appraisal reveals most relationships in the church are shallow at best.

Here's what I intend to teach my children regarding the dinner table.

Oh how I pray you and your family will gather around the dinner table on a regular basis. In fact, I told your mom many years ago that if I could purchase one thing for each of you when you get married it would be a nice dinner table and chairs that you can make memories at.

The Dinner Table • Parenting

Some of my fondest memories were made sitting around our dinner table. I can close my eyes and still envision you all giggling and laughing about some of the strangest things at our table. It was at that table that we laughed together, and occasionally cried. It was where we grew closer as a family. And most importantly, it was around that table that we had serious discussions and grew closer to God.

The inspired psalmist penned these words in Psalm 128:

Blessed *is* every one who fears the Lord, who walks in His ways.
When you eat the labor of your hands, you *shall* be happy,
and it *shall* be well with you.

Your wife *shall* be like a fruitful vine in the very heart of your house,
Your children like olive plants all around your table.
Behold, thus shall the man be blessed who fears the Lord.
The Lord bless you out of Zion, and may you see the good of Jerusalem
All the days of your life. Yes, may you see your children's children.
Peace *be* upon Israel!

Satan will do his best to convince you that you can just grab something on the go. Don't listen to him. Take the time to eat together, play games together, laugh and love together. But do more than that. Invite friends over for meals and fellowship. Make an effort to invite your church family to come eat around your table. In doing that you will learn more about them. You will rejoice and weep with them. You will enjoy one another's fellowship. And you will truly become a church family.

Yes, you can always grab something quick at a drive-thru. But I hope in the years to come that I get to sit around your table and listen to the laughter of my grandchildren as they share funny stories around your table. I love you all very much.

Verses for Further Study

Psalm 128

118

Evolution

Decades ago the problem was more of a minor irritation. Evolution was mentioned in classrooms, but teachers often voiced their own beliefs in the Biblical account of Creation or they skipped the section entirely. Fast forward to the modern "no child left behind" era of standardized testing and atheistic lawsuits, and we find the pendulum has shifted to an environment that is predominantly teaching man's origins from organic evolution. The church sounded the alarm, and we occasionally hear sermons on the topic, but the fact remains that we are still years behind. While we are busy pointing out the lies of evolution in science books, textbook publishers have now shifted the topic into just about every academic field: math, English, home economics, history, etc.

Combine three decades of vigorous teaching in textbooks and spotlights from the mainstream media, and you begin to see why many have fallen prey to this godless theory. (And make no doubt about it, at its root is a theory that all creatures evolved from a common ancestor which itself came from a non-living source—without any plan or design from a Supernatural Creator.) Having preached all over the United States, I have met literally hundreds of Christian parents whose children have left home with a belief in God, only to return months later with an allegiance to evolutionary science. This theory is so prevalent that many Christians today have tried to marry both evolution and the Creation account. Church leaders don't want to feel ignorant, and so they allow Bible class teachers to indoctrinate members with concepts like the Day-Age Theory or the Gap Theory.

Here is what I intend to teach my children about evolution.

Evolution is true — that is, microevolution is true. We know today that things can change within limited parameters (e.g., dog breeds). This is a scientific fact. However, science has never observed a dog reproducing into a fern or giraffe or anything other than a dog. Macro - or organic evolution, on the other hand, the theory that everything evolved from a common ancestor, is unbiblical and unscientific. And while many teachers and professors will try their best to use intellectual intimidation to convince you that all knowledgeable people believe evolution, the fact remains that it is illogical and irrational.

When I first sat down to consider what I would tell you in a single short article regarding evolution, I laughed, as **I could easily fill a book with solid evidence**. However, if I were to try to distill it down, here are some key points I would expect you to know:

1. Evolution cannot explain the existence of matter.

2. Evolution cannot explain how nature progressed from gases and non-living rocks to living material.

3. Evolution cannot explain how the first cell self-assembled (especially in light of the fact that the 2nd Law of Thermodynamics states things are going to a state of increased disorder).

4. Evolution cannot explain the existence of separate male and female genders.

5. Evolution cannot explain human emotions (love, tears, etc.)

6. Evolution cannot explain the division between plants and animal (e.g., why can plants make their own energy through photosynthesis and animals can't?)

7. Evolution cannot explain morality.

8. Evolution cannot explain the design found in nature and the human body. (Design always demands a designer).

9. Evolution cannot explain the sudden explosion and diversity of fossils that appear fully formed in the fossil record.

10. Evolution cannot explain polystrate fossils that completely undermine the geologic column.

11. Evolution cannot explain soft-tissue in dinosaur fossils.

12. Evolution cannot explain the origin of language and consciousness.

The evolutionary theory provides those who have stiffened their necks against God a worldview that excludes a supernatural Creator. If Genesis 1-11 is tossed aside as merely a mythological story, then we must toss out the entire Bible because the one major theme that is taught throughout the Bible is redemption. G. Richard Culp summed it up well when he wrote, "One who doubts the Genesis account will not be the same man he once was, for his attitude toward Holy Scripture has been eroded by false teaching. Genesis is repeatedly referred to in the New Testament, and it cannot be separated from the total Christian message" (1975, pp. 160-161). While men may occasionally grab 2 Peter 3:8 and claim that a day is a thousand years to God, they have done so by taking that passage out of context. As Guy N. Woods pointed out, this passage simply means that time does not affect the performance of God's promises or threats (Woods, 1976, p. 146). The context is when Jesus will return, not how long it took to create the heavens and earth.

Honest Bible scholars will admit that only four books in the Bible do not refer back to the opening chapters of Genesis as **real and historic:** Jude, Philemon, 2 and 3 John. Does this fact mean all other books in the Bible should be cut out or not trusted? Should Christians place their allegiance in evolution? **Absolutely not**—indeed the two theories are at war with one another! A true New Testament Christian realizes the two are incompatible.

Verses for Further Study

Genesis 1-11

Evolution • Christian Family Life

Retirement

It is hard for me to comprehend that some of the individuals I went to school with are already either contemplating retirement or already retired. The reason it is hard for me to grasp that is not because of the money required to make such a step, but rather because they are so young! Each successive generation is trying harder and harder to retire earlier and earlier. There have been countless books written to help individuals workless and retire sooner.

Even within the church we have elevated retirement to something that is honorable and something to which we should all aspire. We fill up our 401k's and we diversify our mutual funds so that our nest eggs will be ready and waiting when that special day comes. But do we really have the right attitude toward our golden years? Or have we embraced a secular worldview when it comes to retirement?

Here is what I intend to teach my children about retirement.

I pray you will erase the word retirement from your vocabulary, forever. Oh, I fully recognize there may be careers that mandate retirement, and there are certain jobs that you will not be able to physically perform when you are older. But I want you to get rid of the idea that you should work hard early in life so you can put your feet up and live a life of ease later on. This is not what our society will tell you, but remember, we never take our cues from the world. Slothfulness, whether at the front end of life or back end of life is unacceptable. While this concept of retiring to "enjoy the golden years" has completely choked out modern society, it was not the original plan.

Before Eve was even fashioned, God had already assigned Adam to work, "Then the Lord God took the man and put him in the garden of Eden to tend and keep it"(Genesis 2:15). God expected man to be a steward of His creation. Adam was to tend the garden in such a way that it brought honor and glory to God. Had Adam not sinned, he

122

Retirement • Christian Family Life

would still be working today. Let me say that again to make sure you didn't miss it: Adam was expected to work, and would still be working if he were alive today.

But that's not all. In Genesis 3, we find God punishing man for sin: "Both thorns and thistles it shall bring forth for you, and you shall eat the herb of the field. **In the sweat of your face** you shall eat bread till you return to the ground, for out of it you were taken; for dust you are, and to dust you shall return" (Genesis 3:18-19, **emp. added**). Notice it was not work that changed, but rather the difficulty of the work. Do we ever read of Biblical figures retiring as our society does today? How about the Apostles? Did they retire and start tooling around in an R.V. in their later years?

A true investigation of Genesis chapter 2 reveals that God prepared both trees that were good to eat, and trees that were pleasing to the eye. It also records that there was gold and onyx stone (2:12). Gold and onyx stone are not needed for gardening. So why were they mentioned? I don't think God intended for man to go out and collect the gold and onyx stone, but rather to use them to glorify Him. Could it be that God provided materials that man could use as he built upon knowledge and began to make tools and other items? (Look at Genesis 4:22).

God created man with the understanding that mankind would work. The Bible uses the words "fellow workers" to describe us (1 Corinthians 3:9). Paul uses this designation frequently to describe faithful Christians (see Romans 16:3,9,21; Philippians 2:25). We are told that those who do not work should not eat (2 Thessalonians 3:10-11). To the church at Ephesus Paul wrote, "Let him who stole steal no longer, but rather let him labor, working with his hands what is good, that he may have something to give him who has need" (Ephesians 4:28).

Lord willing, one day you will become old. Your physical strength will leave you and you will no longer be able to do things you once did. At that point, I encourage you to use your mind and supervise others, imparting your wisdom to them, or write books about what you know. When you get too old to do that, then sit back and share things with younger generations so that they can learn from your triumphs and mistakes. And keep on teaching and sharing until God calls you home!

Verses for Further Study

Genesis 2-3; 4:22	Philippians 2:25
1 Corinthians 3:9	2 Thessalonians 3:10-11
Romans 16:3,9,21	Ephesians 4:28

Mission Minded

What drives an individual to want to pack up all of their belongings and move overseas and work in primitive conditions? Most individuals cannot imagine giving up the thought of having a Wal-Mart less than five miles away, much less living without daily hot showers. And yet, all over the world are individuals who want nothing more than to preach and teach the Word of God. Missionaries. These are individuals who have devoted their lives to taking the Gospel to areas in which the church is weak. These individuals look at the great commission put forth by Jesus Christ and they literally "go": "'Go therefore and make disciples of all the nations, baptizing them in the name of the Father and of the Son and of the Holy Spirit, teaching them to observe all things that I have commanded you; and lo, I am with you always, even to the end of the age.' Amen."

Sadly, for many Christians in the United States, the only true interaction they have with mission work is when someone comes to their local congregation to deliver a mission report. Others sum up their mission experience by writing a check for whoever is currently listed as missionaries on their church bulletin. Mission work is often viewed as something "they" do. Well, who exactly is the "they" and does it include "me?"

Here's what I intend to teach my children regarding mission work.

I'll never forget a devotional that someone led during one of my very first mission trips. While I don't remember the individual who led the devo, his message has remained with me. He used the text from Luke 17:10, "So likewise you, when you have done all those things which you are commanded, say, 'We are unprofitable servants. We have done what was our duty to do.'" His major point in that devotional was that the mission workers on that campaign shouldn't be patting themselves on the back because ultimately we were just doing what we are commanded to do. It totally transformed the way I look at mission work. It's our duty.

You all know that your mom and I put a high value on mission work—both foreign and domestic. We are thankful to be able to support several works and have some dear friends who serve as missionaries. Most of you had a passport before you could walk, as our family would journey off together on mission campaigns. (We still love looking at those early passport photos.) Early on, as we were starting the work of Focus Press, we committed to doing at least one mission campaign per year as a way to give back, for all that the Lord has blessed our family with. It is our prayer that you will follow in our footsteps and support mission work both financially and physically. No matter what your "career" ends up being, you are still expected to be a missionary and servant for God.

One of the biggest obstacles most people have for doing mission work is the rough conditions—whether that be India, Africa, or even being isolated and alone in some New England state. I pray that you never find yourself so married to "stuff" that you are unwilling to "go." Work hard to embrace Isaiah's attitude when he said, "Also I heard the voice of the Lord, saying: 'Whom shall I send, And who will go for Us?' Then I said, 'Here am I! Send me'" (Isaiah 6:8). When an opportunity presents itself, don't look for excuses not to go—rather look for reasons why you should! As you start thinking about your life and how you might get involved in mission areas, let me first encourage you to inspect your heart—and make sure you are doing it for the right reason. Mission work is all about Him and spreading His Word.

Over and over, Scripture reminds us of the importance to spread the good news (which by the way, if you really view it as Good News then you will be more willing to share it!) [See Luke 24:47, Mark 16:15, Acts 13:47, Acts 20:24, etc.] There are many ways this is carried out. Some missionaries take up permanent residence in an area to preach and teach. This is a major commitment in which the individuals spend years in a foreign place. Others conduct short-term missions to specific areas—often going to the same area multiple times. And still others use various forms of media (e.g., radio, print, television) to help spread the Word. I encourage you to get involved in some of these various forms of mission work. Find a work that you are passionate about and devote some time, money, and energy to that work! Do not be satisfied with just sitting in the pew. There is a lady who is eighty years old and still jumps on a plane at least 1-2 times per year to do overseas mission work. Don't make excuses—make it happen!

Occasionally individuals will judge mission works based on

numbers. I think you have been on enough mission campaigns to know the danger in that. In some areas it is easy to baptize individuals by the hundreds—but how many of those remain faithful? In other areas you have to work extremely hard for every single soul! If you ever make it about "numbers" alone, then mission work becomes more like a business. What if the Apostles only went to cities where they could get the biggest return on their time investment?

Finally, when it comes to mission work, I want you to remember that someone loved your dad (and mom) enough to take the time to teach us the Truth. We, in turn, took the time to teach you all. Now continue the tradition — teach others about Him.

Family Discussion

WHAT ARE SOME SIMPLE WAYS YOU CAN BE MISSION MINDED IN YOUR EVERYDAY LIFE?

WHAT IS A BETTER JUDGE OF A SUCCESSFUL MISSION THAN NUMBERS?

Verses for Further Study

Isaiah 6:8	Mark 16:15
Luke 24:47	Acts 13:47; 20:24

The Fear of the Lord

The volume of correspondence I'm receiving from concerned parents regarding their children who have left the church (or are questioning everything) appears to be on the increase. My wife and I have had multiple conversations about why this is happening and what can be done to help. We've reviewed various resources and have offered as much Biblical counsel as we can. Still the letters and emails come.

Apostasy does not discriminate. We have watched as children from "normal" homes, broken homes, affluent homes, and poverty-stricken homes abandon their faith. We have shaken our heads in disbelief over young people who we thought were strong in the faith who are now agnostics or atheists. While there are many variables about why children may be leaving the church, one common denominator that I have discovered is that most of these young people never developed a fear of the Lord.

Years ago, Christians would use the expression "God-fearing" to describe someone who was walking in the light. Today, that expression is rarely heard. I'm afraid that one of the marks of modern Christianity is a casual approach to God and an overall irreverence to Him.

Here's what I intend to teach my children regarding the fear of the Lord.

"The fear of the Lord is the beginning of wisdom; A good understanding have all those who do His commandments" (Psalm 111:10). Look at that again. The beginning of wisdom is having a fear of the Lord. Sure, you may go to school and gain some worldly knowledge. But the fear of the Lord is the beginning of wisdom (see also Proverbs 1:7)! The fear of the Lord is a central issue that if you miss you will not have a solid foundation for your spiritual life.

Let me start by saying there is not enough space for me to really cover this topic as I would like. There are more than 100 pertinent

127

passages on the fear of the Lord, so in this letter I will only touch the hem of the garment (e.g., Proverbs 14:27, Proverbs 3:7, Psalm 86:11, Psalm 19:9, Deuteronomy 31:12, Psalm 112:1). But I'm convinced that part of my job as a father is to help you develop a healthy amount of fear in God. If you grow up not fearing God then I have failed. That is one reason I demand respect and lead you with authority in our home. It is also one of the reasons I discipline you. Because I know that one day you will leave home and be under your heavenly father—and I want you to have a proper relationship with Him. I want you to respect His authority and understand fully that He will punish those who disobey Him.

There are a lot of Christians (and even some preachers) who will cringe at this letter. There are those who have bought into the lie that we should present only the "love and grace" of God. These are the same individuals who are afraid if we come across too strong in our sermons it will run people off. Thus, they have recast God in their lessons as some grandfatherly like figure with a white beard who will never get too upset with anyone. I'm afraid this "cotton candy" preaching is part of the overall problem, and why many young people do not think religion (or God) is relevant to their lives anymore.

Yes, I want you to fear the Lord. A God that can create the universe, create life, and control the weather should humble you and make you fear. We discover the concept of fearing the Lord literally from Genesis to Revelation. In Genesis 31:42 Jacob declares, "Unless the God of my father, the God of Abraham and *the Fear of Isaac*, had been with me ..."(emp. added, see also verse 53). God calls Himself "the Fear of Isaac." God's name reveals a great deal about His character, and yet, in this passage He describes Himself as Fear of Isaac. In Exodus 18 as they are looking for judges to assist Moses we find, "Moreover you shall select from all the people able men, *such as fear God*, men of truth, hating covetousness;" (18:21, emp. added).

After delivering what we often refer to as the Ten Commandments, notice what Moses said to the people, "Do not fear; for God has come to test you, and that *His fear* may be before you, so that you may not sin" (Exodus 20:20, emp. added). When Moses addressed that second generation of Israelites God said, "'Gather the people to Me, and I will let them hear My words, that they may learn to fear Me all the days they live on the earth, and *that* they may teach their children.'" (Deuteronomy 4:10). Do you remember what Solomon wrote after tasting everything this world had to offer: "Let us hear the conclusion of the whole matter: Fear God and keep His commandments, For this is man's all" (Ecclesiastes 12:13). It does not get much clearer than that.

Some might argue that the "God of the New Testament" is not like that. I would remind them that the God of the Old Testament is the same God as the God of the New Testament! Consider Matthew 10:28, "And do not fear those who kill the body but cannot kill the soul. But rather fear Him who is able to destroy both soul and body in hell." Look at Luke 1:50, "And His mercy is on those who fear Him From generation to generation" (see also 1 Peter 2:17). The day you find yourself not fearing the Lord is the day you have gotten "too big for your britches." Humble yourself in His sight.

How do I want you to fear God? Look at the disciples' response on that stormy night in the sea. There they were afraid they were about to drown. They awoke Jesus and He calmed the storm. Yet, instead of rejoicing and celebrating the peaceful seas notice their response: "They were terrified and asked each other, 'Who is this? Even the wind and waves obey him!'" (Mark 4:41). They were in a reverent awe. Think about that when you get up to lead a prayer or wait on the Lord's Table. Never forget what the psalmist wrote: "Let all the earth fear the Lord; Let all the inhabitants of the world stand in awe of Him."

Family Discussion

WHAT ARE SOME HEALTHY FEARS WE HAVE IN OUR LIVES?

WHY IS IT GOOD TO FEAR SOME THINGS?

Verses for Further Study

Proverbs 3:7; 14:27	Ecclesiastes 12:13
Psalm 19:9; 86:11; 112:1	Matthew 10:28
Deuteronomy 4:10; 31:12	Luke 1:50
Genesis 18:21; 31:42, 53	1 Peter 2:17
Exodus 20:20	Mark 4:41

The Fear of the Lord • Christian Family Life

Leaving the Church

In the past decade parents have shared countless stories of their children leaving the faith—so many that they have begun to blur together in my mind. There is the woman whose daughter dated a young man who took her away from the church, and then having accomplished removing her from the church he left her. There is the man who literally had to sit down for several minutes and catch his breath he was crying so hard revealing that two of his children were now lost. There are so many... (I wish I had written them down and kept a journal). There were children who never really engaged in the first place, and then there were those who were active in everything the church offered, but the ending of the story is the same. They are now lost. It's the elephant in the room that we don't talk about. In every congregation I visit there are couples who know the pain of a lost child (or children). Oh, we all know the elephant exists, but maybe if we don't mention its presence, it will go away.

While many leaders and preachers in the church refuse to admit there is a problem, the evidence is right before our noses each week. In fact, in many congregations there is a complete missing generation of Christians in their 20s. The elephant is not going away. Instead, our lack of addressing the situation and looking for real solutions is only making the elephant grow bigger. We continue to do the same exact thing, expecting a different result. Because after all, if we talk about it then some might feel we are "judging" their past parenting choices. Or worse, they may leave the church building feeling sad.

It is time we wake up, church! It is time we admit the old system is broken. And it is time we as a body of believers roll up our sleeves and look for realistic solutions.

***Here's what I intend to teach my children
regarding leaving the church.***

I can assure you that on at least a few occasions there will be times when you question whether you want to be associated with the church. For instance:

It may be when the preacher forgets to visit you when you are in the hospital.

It may be when no flowers RE sent when one of your relatives dies.

It may be when someone says something very hurtful in the foyer.

It may be when someone pushes you out of their "area" like the audio/visual booth because that is "their domain."

It may be when a youth minister talks condescendingly to you as a parent.

It may be when your preacher begins repeating sermons because of lack of preparation.

It may be when an elder begins to "lord" his position over the flock.

It may be when the congregation splits over personalities and emotions.

It may be when a new preacher arrives who for whatever reason doesn't warm up to your family.

It may be when a deacon dismisses your ideas and suggestions.

It may be when you feel like the congregation has grown cold and sterile.

It may be when you feel like every one is in a clique and you are always on the outside looking in.

It may be when a song leader refuses to sing songs you love to sing.

It may be when a Christian borrows something and never returns it.

It may be when the eldership gives in to the desires of some of the members rather than standing up for what is right.

It may be when your children are hurt because of the actions of others.

But whatever the reason, ***never ever leave the church!*** God had a perfect plan before the foundation of the world (1 Peter 1:20; Ephesians 1:4; see also 2 Timothy 1:8-9). Here is the reality—God designed a perfect church and Jesus Christ founded it. However, that church is comprised of imperfect people. Some of those people will hurt you. Some may let you down. Others may stir up feelings of anger. But never forget that you too are imperfect. You will, on occasion, let others down. You will also hurt people and may cause feelings of anger.

You have witnessed first-hand the sadness and hurt that your mom and I feel each time we hear about someone we know who has children who have left the church. The very thought of it rocks us to our core, and reminds us once again what our job on this earth truly is. Understand that should you ever make the decision to leave, I will not just watch you go. I will be by your side teaching, crying, admonishing,

Leaving the Church • Christian Family Life

131

and when necessary, rebuking you, in an effort to bring you back. I will encourage your siblings to reach out to you in love and help bring you back as well. I will not rest until you are back in the fold. When I finally lay down to take my last breath, the only thing I really want to think about in that moment is that my children (and grandchildren) are all faithful—and thus I will see them again one day soon.

As you seek to find your place in the body, you need to do all you can to get along with those around you. Paul admonished, "I, therefore, the prisoner of the Lord, beseech you to walk worthy of the calling with which you were called, with all lowliness and gentleness, with longsuffering, bearing with one another in love, endeavoring to keep the unity of the Spirit in the bond of peace" (Ephesians 4:1-3). Find your place in the body and get busy serving Him rather than focusing on all the imperfections around you.

Family Discussion

WHAT IS SOMETHING YOU CAN DO TO GUARD AGAINST ANY FUTURE DESIRES TO LEAVE THE CHURCH?

HOW CAN YOU INCLUDE OTHERS IN YOUR PREVENTATIVE PLAN?

Verses for Further Study

1 Peter 1:20	2 Timothy 1:8-9
Ephesians 1:4	Ephesians 4:1-3

Identifying the Enemy

In Romans 7:21-25, Paul describes a battle going on within himself. While his mind knows and wants to obey the law of God, there is another law "in the members of my body, waging war against the law of my mind and making me a prisoner of the law of sin which is in my members" (v. 23). Consider for a moment that this is the apostle Paul speaking, and yet he revealed that he still has this war going on in his flesh. If Paul faced this challenge, then modern Christians will too.

While we comprehend this battle, most pulpits focus only on the remedy — that if you sin, you will be forgiven — but they remain silent on God's original design. The design is that we are saved **to be holy and reflect Christ.** What many hear is "you're forgiven" and they go right on sinning. In neglecting the design we are only preaching a portion of the Gospel — and not transforming ourselves into the image of Christ. Rarely do we meditate on what we are doing to Christ and God's original plan for man.

Here's what I intend to teach my children regarding the ugliness of sin.

In chapter three of the famous Chinese general Sun Tzu's book The Art of War on military strategy, Tzu reminds readers of the importance of knowing your enemy. He says you must know both the enemy and yourself or you will not win. As we translate his advice into the spiritual battle going on inside us, the first thing you must do is recognize the enemy — sin.

Understand that Satan will do all he can to camouflage sin as acceptable or good. A fish would never bite down on a naked hook— so a fisherman hides the hook behind spinners and shiny things to distract the fish. The hook is still there. Likewise, Satan tries to veil sin by every conceivable means. He may hide it behind a shiny spinner called worldliness. Or he may disguise the hook and try to hide it in the darkest recesses of your heart. Or he may show you something that is tempting and tell you that you are being too legalistic. But remember—

133

the hook is still there. Learn to look for the hook. If you ever hope to win this battle you must first recognize the enemy. Remember, Paul called it the "law of sin."

Sin is the master of disguise, and that's why you must constantly have your head in the game. Your flesh will be tempted when you are at the top of your game or the bottom. It will hit when you are rich or poor. Remember what James said, "But each one is tempted when he is drawn away by his own desires and enticed. Then, when desire has conceived, it gives birth to sin; and sin, when it is full-grown, brings forth death" (James 1:14-15).

You have a war going on within you. In Galatians Paul declared, "For the flesh lusts against the Spirit, and the Spirit against the flesh; and these are contrary to one another, so that you do not do the things that you wish" (Galatians 5:17). My prayer is that early in your life you will recognize the enemy and you will use whatever means necessary (silver bullet, stake through the heart, kryptonite, etc.) to kill this monster. I want you to reach the point that sin becomes sickening to you—because it is to God. It will not happen overnight. It will be a lifelong battle that may on occasion leave you weary. But never forget you have Jesus on your side, and therefore you will reign victorious in the end.

When you are baptized your sins are washed away—but that cleansing came at the ultimate cost of God's Son. Unfortunately, sin re-enters the picture. Many Christians just rest under the notion that being washed in the blood of Christ means we are forgiven and they do nothing about the new sins that creep up in their lives. Being washed does mean we are forgiven, but God's design was that we would walk on the narrow path (Matthew 7) to reach the narrow gate. Paul wrote, "But put on the Lord Jesus Christ, and make no provision for the flesh, to fulfill its lusts" (Romans 13:14).

In order to fight back, you need to imagine your mind as a watchman for your soul. Do not allow the watchman to become entangled in sin. Proverbs 4:23 records, "Keep your heart with all diligence, for out of it spring the issues of life." Keep a watchful eye for holes in the walls of your fortress where sin might try to get through. To keep your mind sharp and ensure you are winning the battle make yourself meditate on God— on His goodness and His holiness. Out in our back yard, I've designated a couple of large rocks for you to have some alone time to pray and meditate to God. Get into the Word and focus your attention on the things that are pleasing to God. Find time to just get away and talk to God.

Whatsoever things are true, whatsoever things are noble ... (Philippians 4:8). Think on these things.

Verses for Further Study

Romans 7:21-25	Matthew 7	Philippians 4:8
James 1:14-15	Romans 13:14	
Galatians 5:17	Proverbs 4:23	

A Biblical Worldview

Do you want to know what type of worldview your children or grandchildren possess? Ask them this simple question: Do you think God gave specific roles to women or are they equal with men? I will warn you beforehand—you might want to have some aspirin on-hand and a wet rag for your head before you ask this question. Why? Many our of children have bought the lie and have been indoctrinated with a secular worldview.

Society has done an incredible job of communicating the idea that men and women are equal—in every aspect of life. Women are now graduating from the Army Rangers school. Men are constantly bombarded by the mainstream media's message to be less masculine and instead embrace gender neutrality. The world is doing everything it can to instill a worldview in our children in which gender boundaries do not exist, including making bathrooms and locker-rooms gender neutral. But is this concept Biblical? Consider the worldview that promotes this twisted perspective.

Let me state right up front that I know when it comes to salvation and being created in the image of God that men and women are equal. But the Biblical (and scientific) reality is that men and women are different. And truth be told, we have different roles. Just because the secular worldview says we don't does not change the Truth. If we hope to plug the leak of young people leaving the church then one area we must confront head-on is in teaching our children a biblical worldview.

Here's what I intend to teach my children regarding a biblical worldview.

You have never had an official class on worldviews—but I dare say your mother and I have invested more hours on this concept than just about any other subject. We have strived hard to equip you with a biblical worldview. We recognize that we can't cover every single life scenario in the short time you are under our roof. Instead, we have tried to teach you how to look at things through the lens of God's Word. Countless hours have gone into showing you that emotion and opinions ultimately do not matter, but rather Truth can only be found in God's Word.

A biblical worldview does not change because of culture. It is not affected by popular opinion. Instead, a biblical worldview is concerned with constantly evaluating everything though Scripture.

I will warn you ahead of time that many people—even in the church—do not hold to a biblical worldview. Many of these people will look at you as though you have lost your mind, or that you are old-fashioned, or out of touch. In fact, there will be times you will feel pressure or receive negative comments simply because you are encouraging people to follow principles of Scripture rather than going along with the world. Don't give in. Don't take your eyes off of what is Truth.

*A*sk yourself. What is shaping my worldview? Is it something I need to re-evaluate?

Allow me to give you an example from the discussion above regarding gender equality. In order to answer the question, "Do you think God gave specific roles to women or are they equal with men?" we don't turn to our culture or opinion. Instead, we turn to Scripture. In Genesis 2 we recognize man was created first and was given the task of tending the Garden. After discovering Adam was lonely, God created woman from man and brought her to the man, who named her. In Genesis 3 we find Eve being deceived by the serpent and giving the fruit to her husband. We then look at their punishments (Genesis 3:14-19). Notice that part of the woman's curse is that "Your desire shall be for your husband, and he shall rule over you." Those are fighting words for many today—nevertheless they are Truth from God's Word.

In 1 Corinthians 11:3 Paul wrote, "But I want you to know that the head of every man is Christ, the head of woman is man, and the head of Christ is God." So, according to the Bible there is a distinct hierarchy. In 1 Peter 3:7 we read, "Husbands, likewise, dwell with them with understanding, giving honor to the wife, as to the weaker vessel, and as being heirs together of the grace of life, that your prayers may not be hindered." Also according to the Bible women are the weaker vessels. Notice this passage is not saying inferior.

Paul also wrote that older women are to "admonish the young women to love their husbands, to love their children, to be discreet, chaste, homemakers, good, obedient to their own husbands, that the word of God may not be blasphemed" (Titus 2:4-5). He also told Timothy, " Therefore I desire that the younger widows marry, bear children, manage the house, give no opportunity to the adversary to speak reproachfully" (1 Timothy 5:14). Add to these passages qualifications for elders and deacons and you begin to see very specific differences (1 Timothy 5; Titus 1).

So in answering the question, "Do you think God gave specific roles to women or are they equal with men?" the answer is a resounding yes! God did give specific roles. (Likewise He gave specific roles to men!) Additionally, according to Scripture we are different. This doesn't mean one is better than the other. But according to Scripture we are different—and therefore should act differently. Again, possessing a Biblical worldview is not popular. It will probably cause people to believe you are weird. But remember, our task is to be followers of God rather than followers of man.

Verses for Further Study

Genesis 2; 3:14-19	1 Peter 3:7	1 Timothy 5
1 Corinthians 11:3	Titus 2:4-5	Titus 1

Feeding Your Soul

Satan is real, and he knows how to keep humans preoccupied with things that ultimately don't matter much. Humans spend countless hours enjoying things like sports, crafts, and various hobbies. While these things are not wrong in and of themselves, they can often take our focus away from things of eternal importance. Sadly, in our culture, these activities are so popular that most Christians never question them or consider how much time they devote to such activities. As a result, many Christians are physically fit and talented at their hobbies, but they are starving spiritually.

Sadly, many congregations feed this problem. Rather than digging deeper into the Word, congregations will plan fluffy and fun activities that entertain. Rather than feeding the flock, many elderships have become masters at entertaining the flock and keeping them busy. All the while, our congregations get spiritually weaker as souls starve for the Word.

Here's what I intend to teach my children regarding feeding their souls.

One of the toughest things I can teach you is how to "stand." In discussing putting on the whole armor of God, Paul wrote, "Therefore take up the whole armor of God, that you may be able to withstand in the evil day, and having done all, to stand. Stand therefore, ..." (Ephesians 6:13-14). Paul stressed the importance of being able to stand. My job is to teach you how to stand, even when culture is trying to push you in a different direction.

There will be many times in your life that you feel like a salmon swimming upstream going against current, while all the other fish are swimming downstream. Your friends may fill their lives up with sports activities or become obsessed with hobbies. Stand—and feed your soul.

God did not create you to simply be on this planet and have fun.

Feeding Your Soul • Christian Family Life

Many people try to fill the void in their lives with hobbies and entertainment. But the only thing that can truly fill you is when you feed your soul.

If you find your life too busy, please get into His Word and grow. I hear many sermons and many people talking about getting into God's Word—but few actually take the time to dig deeply. Spend time observing God's creation and praising Him. Spend time reflecting on how small you are in the grand scheme of things and give God thanks. Spend time evaluating your life and the areas you fall short, and confess these weaknesses to Him. Spend time meditating on heaven and spending eternity with Him. Spend more time in prayer, allowing Jesus to intercede on your behalf. Spend time lamenting on those who are sick or suffering and look for ways to help them. In other words, feed your soul!

Let me encourage you, set aside the media that is trying to invade your lives and fellowship with others. Sit around a table with some friends and enjoy fellowshipping with them. Take meals to those who are shut-in or sick. Spend time sitting with them or listening to them talk about "the good old days." Turn off the television and open your home up for Bible studies. In other words, feed your soul.

Look for ways to do good to others. Reach out to those who may be hurting financially. Join hands with those who are building homes for the less fortunate. Take time to do mission work. Get out and knock on doors or teach at a VBS. Feed your soul.

I should caution you that if you heed my advice, you will find hobbies and sports do not fulfill you the way they used to—your heart will long for something more. You will crave real connections and activities that have a deeper purpose. You will begin to look at things differently. You will be actively living the life Christ intended you to live! So look for ways to feed your soul!

Verses for Further Study
Ephesians 6:13-14

Absolute Truth

I was conducting an open Question and Answer session when an audience member responded, "We can't know the truth with any certainty." The most troubling part of this comment was that the young person making the claim believed it 100 percent. I should not have been surprised, as concepts like post-modernism and enlightenment have been with us for decades now. Society has done a phenomenal job teaching young people that there is no black and white—but rather everything is a lovely shade of gray.

There is a generation coming up that believes the only real reality is what they themselves have experienced, and that feelings trump everything. This is the same generation who has been indoctrinated with the idea that evolutionary science is the only form of knowledge, and that science is eternal. They firmly believe knowledge/truth produced by science (by the rational objective knowing self) will always lead toward progress and perfection. Furthermore, they have been taught that anyone who declares a standard for truth that is not based on feelings or science is intolerant and hateful.

As a result, many parents and preachers have backed away from declaring things absolutely black and white. We no longer use phrases like absolute truth. In the 1970's people accused Christians of thinking they were the only ones going to heaven—and that they believed everyone else was going to hell. Instead of using a balanced approach to respond to that, most pulpits shifted the pendulum all the way to the other side and no longer spoke of hell, the uniqueness of the church, or the fact that Jesus founded only one church. I fear we are doing the same today with truth. We have moved the pendulum and instead of giving a balanced response we no longer talk in terms of what does the Bible say, but rather how does that make you feel?

Here's what I intend to teach my children regarding absolute truth.

There are many things that are absolutely right or absolutely wrong and your feelings have nothing to do with it. Truth does not come from your emotions, your heart, or what you've experienced (Jeremiah 17:9). The Bible says very plainly, "Sanctify them by Your truth. Your word is truth." (John 17:17). The inspired psalmist proclaimed, "The entirety of Your word is truth, and every one of Your righteous judgments endures forever" (Psalm 119:160). What these passages tell us is that real truth comes from God. In fact, God is referred to in Scripture as the God of Truth (Psalm 31:5).

Many things like the media or textbooks will try to persuade you into adopting their secular hedonistic worldview of truth. Satan will do all he can to extinguish your biblical worldview—and to make you rely on your feelings. However, spend some time studying passages like Psalm 108. In this psalm of praise, the inspired psalmist declares, "I will praise You, O LORD, among the peoples, and I will sing praises to You among the nations. For Your mercy is great above the heavens, and Your truth reaches to the clouds (Psalm 108:3-4). In describing God, Psalm 146:6 records that it is He, "Who made heaven and earth, the sea and all that is in them. Who keeps truth forever."

When you read passages like Proverbs 6, which lists specific things God hates, it doesn't mean these are bad if you agree. Those are things that our immutable God has always and will always hate and view as an abomination. That is an absolute Truth. Just like when God makes a covenant with man. That is an absolute Truth! Remember God cannot lie (Titus 1:2; Hebrews 6:18). Man can and does—but God cannot lie.

It is not wrong or hateful to stand for absolute truths. Do not be afraid to declare the Truth! Make sure you always proclaim the truth in love (Ephesians 4:15), but we don't ever need to compromise the truth because someone's feelings may get hurt. Remember, God's Word will prick the heart of those who are lost. Rather than asking people what they believe is true, spend your time instilling God's truths in your heart (Deuteronomy 11:18). And never forget the words of Jesus when He declared: "I am the way, the truth, and the life. No one comes to the Father except through Me" (John 14:6).

Verses for Further Study

Jeremiah 17:9	Psalm 119:160	Hebrews 6:18
John 14:6; 17:17	Proverbs 6	Ephesians 4:15
Psalm 31:5; 108	Titus 1:2	Deut. 11:18

Absolute Truth • Christian Family Life

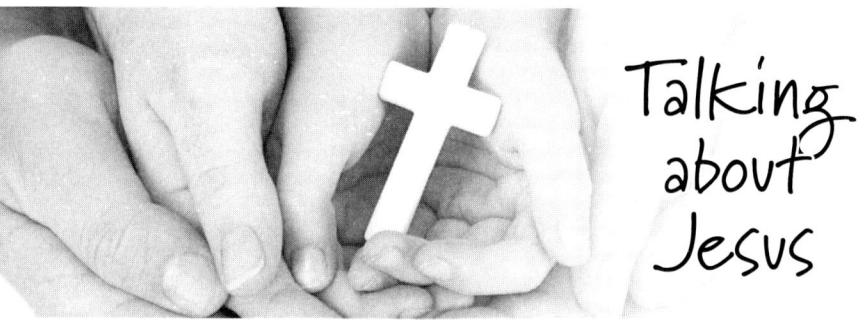

Talking about Jesus

Do you want to know what someone is really passionate about? Spend just an hour listening to them talk and you will quickly discover their passion. Maybe it's their career. Or maybe they are passionate about decorating and having just the right "Magnolia" Fixer Upper look. Or maybe they are passionate about their children or their golf game. Whatever it is, sooner or later that person will talk about it—and when they do, you can almost see their face light up, as they begin chatting away.

It is somewhat distressing to me that Christians—who are supposed to be passionate about Jesus Christ—don't talk about Him more often. Sure, we may occasionally talk about something that was mentioned in a sermon or we may even offer a "God bless you" when someone sneezes. But the reality is we often don't talk about our Savior very much in public. And when we do, it is usually guarded and with a great deal of reservation.

I have heard from literally dozens of Christians, who are troubled by the fact that their denominational friends talk about Jesus and religious matters more openly than most New Testament Christians. Yes, we believe He is the way, the truth, and the life (John 14:6), but sadly we don't bring Him up in everyday conversation.

Here's what I intend to teach my children regarding talking about Jesus.

Let me start by admitting I don't know the precise history on this one, but my understanding—having talked to many faithful Christians—is that more than fifty years ago there was a concerted effort for New Testament Christians to separate themselves from the Pentecostal movement. Pentecostals were viewed as those "Holy Rollers" who spoke in tongues, raised their hands, clapped during worship, and often talked about being filled with the spirit. In an effort to separate us from them, New Testament Christians shifted the

Talking about Jesus • Christian Family Life

143

pendulum all the way to the other side and avoided anything that could even remotely be viewed as being Pentecostal.

In doing so, many members of the church stopped openly talking about their faith and stopped talking about Jesus. Oh sure, we would occasionally talk about doctrine, but we didn't want to be viewed as weird or one of "them." And so we grew silent. Here's my first piece of advice about this one: Don't be afraid to talk about Jesus. After all, if we are passionate about Him and want to share the truth with others, then we should feel good talking about Him.

Second, get comfortable talking about Him when you are young. If it becomes a part of your everyday speech then you won't feel awkward later on in life trying to fit Him into your conversations. Part of being ready and able to give a defense of the hope that is in you (1 Peter 3:15) is being able to talk about Jesus.

Third, never ever forget the confession you made at your baptism (Acts 8:37), and do not fear confessing Him to anyone. I want you to soberly consider what Jesus said: "Therefore whoever confesses Me before men, him I will also confess before My Father who is in heaven. But whoever denies Me before men, him I will also deny before My Father who is in heaven" (Matthew 10:32-33). I believe many people deny Him by simply remaining silent and not defending Him and His teachings.

Later on Paul wrote to the Christians in Rome and declared, "If you confess with your mouth the Lord Jesus and believe in your heart that God has raised Him from the dead, you will be saved. For with the heart one believes unto righteousness, and with the mouth confession is made unto salvation" (Romans 10:9-10). Notice that with the mouth confession is made unto salvation.

Does that sound like Paul wants people to be timid or shy about Jesus?

Understand that in talking openly about Jesus some people may be offended. Try to be respectful and kind, but also keep in mind the desperate need they have for His cleansing blood. Additionally, you may make some Christians uncomfortable by openly talking about Jesus. They may not be used to hearing someone talk freely about Christ and their appreciation for Him. But stop and think about what that really says about their beliefs and their love for Him.

Do you really love Jesus? Are you thankful for what He did for you on the cross? Then don't be afraid to shout it from the mountains or talk about it on the subway! Who knows, it might just open some doors for you to talk to others about Him.

Family Discussion

IS IT INTIMIDATING OR UNCOMFORTABLE FOR YOU TO THINK OF TALKING TO OTHERS ABOUT JESUS? IF SO ASK YOURSELF WHY THAT IS.

WHAT WAYS COULD TALKING ABOUT JESUS HELP YOU STRENGTHEN YOUR FAITH?

Verses for Further Study

John 14:6	Acts 8:37	Romans 10:9-10
1 Peter 3:15	Matthew 10:32-33	

Talking about Jesus • Christian Family Life